The stories written by Shashanka Ghosh make for pleasant reading. Over the years, he has evolved a style of his own to catch the essence of every day middle class Indian life. While writing stories, Shashanka weaves the weal and woe of the persons who have reached the twilight years of their lives. In some of the stories, the ending comes as a blow of sledge hammer which makes the works very dramatic, hence interesting and rewarding.

Writing is not the vocation of Shashanka, but as a reader I want to be delighted with more helpings.

Nandita Basu

Writer, Member – Comparative Literature Association India, Phd, ex HOD University of Delhi

Some Broken Hearts

SHASHANKA GHOSH

First Published in April 2023

ISBN: 978-93-5741-281-0

BLUEROSE PUBLISHERS

www.BlueRoseONE.com

info@bluerosepublishers.com

+91 8882 898 898

Cover Design:

Shashanka Ghosh

Illustration Design:

Pooja Bishnoi

Typographic Design:

Rohit

Distributed by: BlueRose, Amazon, Flipkart

To baba....
Who loved to read

Introduction

Fiction, some argue does not exit. And I reluctantly agree. It may not be true but then it is a perspective from which to view fiction.

If you pick any of the twelve stories, you would notice the stark similarity or rather an absence of dissimilarity between them and our general view of life, our environment in life or people around us.

Though I can safely bet that each story sprouts from the parched well of my imagination, it breaths with life only by drawing from life happening around us.

This book is about us, we humans and our mundane, trivial matters of survival.

Normally we react to what life throws at us, weak in the face of challenges, be it in our relationships, in our workplace and above all in dealing with our fear, our insecurities, etc.

In ' *The Unspoken Distance*', the tussle between a doting mother and her feisty child is not uncommon. However hard each tries, to truly give in to love every time would always remain a struggle.

In 'Cheesy Love', with rather unconventional characters, the reader, I bet would be able to sympathize with the scurrying paws and for some identify with the mischievous couple.

The fear every child deals with when facing an overbearing father as in 'The stolen Pride' cannot be overstated. Why can't fathers be more like mothers? Compassionate, soft, approachable, the list can go on. Why? I don't know. Maybe they really are from Mars. Maybe they are scared to display their vulnerability. Maybe they think it's the only path to discipline the child. But that is how it is and the child is not evolved in dealing with it in any other way than the way he deals with it, with fear. And two decades later that fear shapes an insecure father who is incapable of effectively dealing with his confused son.

'Companions', 'Cheesy Love', 'Unrequited Love', 'The Instinctive Couple' and 'The Sober Love' are various hues of love and relationships that colour our lives.

'Mirage' takes a cue from our present day issue and a serious one, to disseminate awareness about severe water scarcity looming over the horizon in the coming decades. Imagine the world of turmoil, misery and eventual extermination if, God forbid, we reach that stage. The very thought sends a tingle down my spine.

The stories have been woven with a lot of musings and I am sure reveals your taste and mine.

Enjoy the stories and even if you get serious at the end and ponder for a moment, remember it is just a story ...yours and mine.

Shashanka Ghosh

Contents

The Fishy Smell

Sunday Morning

The smile on Shamol's face was contagious. He surveyed the laid out fishes, strolling from one vendor to another. A row of fishmongers perched on a raised rectangular platform that was tailored to a perfect height for patrons to explore with ease. Each vendor presented an array of fish, thoughtfully segregated by species and neatly arranged on banana leaves that were spread out on gleaming circular aluminum trays. Some sellers arranged their catch directly on banana leaves before them, sans containers. The bustling alley between the platforms were crammed with enthusiastic fish connoisseurs in various hues, eagerly bargaining, haggling, jostling, observing and exploring before finally selecting their prized catch.

Garihat fish market was one of the largest in Kolkata and Shamol was familiar with every nook and cranny.

"You look very happy today Shamolda, what's the matter?" asked Bappi as he split a fish head into two with his *Boti*, a curved blade, pointed at one end and clamped to a wooden base which was firmly held in position by his feet. 'Da' prefixed by

Bappi before Shamol's name was a generic term for elderly respect. Several customers patiently stood in a row for their turn. On normal days, Bappi dealt with customers and counted the cash while his assistant would clean, chop and pack the fish. However, on Sunday mornings, with the market brimful, the frenzy kept them both hard-pressed.

Bappi and Shamol cherished a bond of fifty years, from the day a young kid walked in to buy fish with his father for the first time while a younger Bappi sat alongside his Dad.

"Samrat is coming in a couple of days; on Tuesday," the excitement in his voice was evident. At seventy, Shamol's frame was erect. His thick lustrous hair, albeit silvery, was well oiled and neatly parted. Clean-shaven with high cheekbones and smooth tanned skin, he looked a decade younger.

"This time, he is coming after many days," said Bappi without looking up, remembering Samrat as a young lad of seven, following his father everywhere in the fish market, the timid Samrat.

"Yes, after two years as he was occupied and could not afford leave due to Covid. His green card could have been terminated if he got stuck here." Shamol justified.

"So, it has to be *hilsa* today, right?" smiled Bappi as he dipped his arms into a small iron bucket that lay by his side. He wore a tight thin-strapped brown vest, stained with blood at several spots and a loose white pajama.

"How much?" asked Shamol.

"Take a big one. After all, Samrat is coming after a long time and it is his favorite. For you - thousand for a kg, though you won't get it for less than twelve hundred anywhere in the market," Bappi offered plainly.

Shamol knew Bappi was right. Though the price required his meager budget to stretch, his only son was coming from the USA after a long time and serving a common fish was unimaginable. *Hilsa*, once a regular necessity, had become a luxury due to supply shortage and price hitting the roof. In fact, Shamol was mortified to go to the fish market. For a fish lover, *Hilsa*, which melts in the mouth like soft butter when steamed in mustard paste, epitomized ultimate delicacy. For a proud Bengali, to rein in the pack of disgruntled and disparaging tongues, it was imperative to serve the fish during any function, no matter what the price. *Hilsa* remains a status symbol.

"I brought some *Hilsa*…. for Samrat. We will prepare it with mustard for Lunch on Thursday," said Shamol, handing over the polybag to his wife. Ruma was an unassuming, God-fearing woman who believed in relishing the small pleasures of life. Seeing a smile on her loved ones, tending her flowerpots or waking with the sun to feel the morning dew on her skin was her idea of a miracle and it perennially reminded her of her good fortune to be a part of this enchanting mystery called life.

"You could have bought *Rohu* or *Bhetki*," said Ruma indifferently as she clutched her right knee to rise. The pain was becoming unbearable and her plump figure further accentuated the affliction. "After migrating he has lost interest in fish. He prefers KFC or McDonalds," said Ruma. She shook her head to register her disapproval.

Shamol knew Ruma was the more prudent and practical between them - always has been. *'My boy will definitely crave for fish this time,'* he was sure.

Hello Baba, sorry for not keeping in touch for some time. Was busy. I will land in Kolkata on Tuesday morning. There is something important to discuss. See U. Love, Samy.

It was the seventeenth time Shamol went through the message on his botched mobile, which had got him excited since Saturday evening.

"Why does he call himself Samy? Samrat is such a royal name, king of kings," Shamol wondered to himself as he did whenever he came across the shortened version.

"And what does he want to discuss? I will tell him to get me a smartphone this time." Shamol was always embarrassed to take out his phone in public. The black cell phone was old; it was a base model that Samrat had gifted him some years back. The paint, from extensive use, had eroded at several spots causing the edges and back flap to turn silvery; some numbers were illegible and the gadget entailed tying with several rubber bands to hold it together.

Monday Morning

"Baba, are we buying Hilsa today?" asked an overexcited Samrat as they entered the Fish market on a bright Sunday morning. The place was crowded with animated fish enthusiasts and loud fish sellers, but there was a certain discipline and vibrancy in the fishy air that captivated the old and young alike, leaving them elated.

"How are you Shamolda?" asked Bappi without looking up. "And how is Samrat today?" Samrat hid behind his father and peeped furtively while unconsciously chewing at the hem of his father's Kurta.

"He is too shy; which fish would you like today? Hilsa? Do you go to school?" asked Bappi, grinning widely to flaunt his betel stained teeth.

"He does," Shamol answered for his son.

"Baba, why is Bappi Uncle always shouting? I am scared of him," asked Samrat on their walk back as he joyfully swung the polybag.

Shamol smiled.

"It's five thirty," Ruma yawned while switching on the bedside lamp. "Why are you smiling like that?" asked Ruma, unmindful that Shamol was still sleeping. "Get up, it's already five thirty."

Shamol's eyes opened with a start.

"So, you were dreaming. Hmmm, what was it about?" asked Ruma, folding the blanket and tidying the sheet on her side of the bed. "Come on, don't be lazy," continued Ruma in the same breath.

Shamol hated rising early, especially during the winters and being dragged by Ruma for their morning breathing exercises followed by Yoga, *'I will get relief from her authority once she is gone'* mused Shamol and immediately regretted the thought.

The thought seemed so loud that he instinctively looked up to see if she was staring angrily at him. He knew he would not survive for long if she went first.

He could not deny that since they had embraced Yoga, he felt more energetic and alive. On days he missed the morning ritual, he would inevitably lack physical and mental agility and the day would drag laboriously.

"Drink your tea, it's already cold," said Ruma. The rustle of the newspaper that covered his face indicated Shamol's nod.

"Shoma, clear the table," yelled Ruma. Breakfast was over and Shamol was idling with his tea.

"I will have the tea, don't take the cup," he said to Shoma before she could sweep the table clean with a swift brush of her hand.

The balmy December day with a cool breeze caressed their skin while the couple was immersed in their world; Shamol, with his newspaper and Ruma, with her knitting, both oblivious and aware of each other. They relished the time of the day, more so during winters when they could sit outside in their small lawn, wet their feet in grass, listen to the bird's chirp and bathe in fresh air.

Shoma's polite call for lunch would eventually break their stupor. At a tender age of sixteen, a few days after Samrat was born, Shoma was sent into their household by Shamol's father-in-law to assist in household work. She did not marry, despite regular insistence by Ruma for several years and chose to be an indispensable member of their family.

Shamol was the proud owner of a bungalow with a modest lawn in one of the upscale localities of Kolkata. During the late

70's, since loan from a bank was a prerogative of the affluent and housing loans were not as rampant or ubiquitous as today, he had taken a loan for the purchase from a private moneylender. High interest accrued on the loan and the Principal amount could finally be repaid a couple of years before Shamol retired from the establishment he served for thirty-five years.

He retired as Head Accountant.

His independent house was a reason for envy among his brother who did not share Shamol's luck or taste or foresight.

"But a bungalow is a bungalow after all," Shamolda would deliberately poke at them and revel in smug satisfaction.

The opening clink of the semicircular lock on the main gate woke Shamol from his reverie. He had dozed off onto one side with the newspaper dangling from his hand.

"Ah ha! Sanjay is here," Ruma smiled and moved towards the gate.

Sanjay was around six feet, well built with a slight paunch that he would consciously try to camouflage under a loose *kurta* or a shirt. His fair face sported a neat French cut while his thick black hair was well groomed. He wore a golden-rimmed round spectacle. He wore a loose turquoise *khadi* half shirt with light blue denims and blue suede shoes.

During his childhood, Sanjay's family occupied the bungalow adjacent to Shamol's. As a child, Sanjay would frequently be found playing with Samrat or fixed on Ruma's lap as she animatedly modulated her voice to narrate an allegory. His eyes still shone with adoration and reverence for Ruma who had never made any discrimination between him and her son.

After his father expired following a stroke, Sanjay sold his bungalow to settle his father's business debts and moved to a smaller apartment on rent.

"What a pleasant surprise, how is my little son?" said Ruma, hugging Moni before her outstretched hand could touch Ruma's feet.

Shamol joined Ruma for the greetings. Shujit immediately bent to touch his feet as a mark of respect, followed by Sanjay.

"How old is Shujit now, six, seven…?" wondered Ruma gently rubbing his hair.

"He will be seven in February, kaki," beamed Moni with a glint of pride in her big eyes.

"Come, come sit. Shoma, get some more chairs, Sanjay is here," shouted Ruma.

Shoma rushed awkwardly balancing three plastic chairs in her outstretched hands and placed them around the round table.

"Kaki," said Sanjay, handing a packet to Shoma.

"What is it?" asked Ruma, peeping into the polybag.

"Little *Rehu*, nothing much," said Sanjay.

"Please sit; and you sit on grandma's lap," said Ruma lovingly and pulled Shujit to her.

"You have come after a long time," complained Shamol to Sanjay, speaking for the first time.

"I know Kaka; there is no explanation; we always think of coming but it does not materialize; we are basically lazy," said Sanjay staring at his wife for approval.

"Say I am lazy; not we are lazy," came the immediate retort.

"Now you guys don't start a fight as usual; Excuse me, I will just check on lunch," smiled Ruma and went inside.

Shujit occupied the big cushioned wooden chair and laid out his arms on the armrests with a broad grin. His thick lustrous hair almost touched his eyes.

"So, Sanjay, how is your work...?" trailed off Shamol without really caring for a reply.

"Why did you cook the *Hilsa*? Don't you know that I had brought it for Samrat; He is coming tomorrow morning; couldn't you wait for another day? You very well know that we cannot afford it," barked an animated and livid Shamol. He was pacing frantically with hands tied behind his back and blood shot eyes that emanated fury.

Ruma expressionlessly stared at him, looking beyond him or maybe through him. She was expecting some drama to erupt after noticing Shamol's grumpy and forced demeanor during lunch. He was monosyllabic during the entire afternoon.

However, Sanjay did not notice Shamol's restiveness. The mind sees what it wants to see and Sanjay has always respected him. Moni sensed something was amiss.

"The little boy loves *Hilsa*, Shamol; Sanjay was here after so long. We cannot serve the fish he brought us. It is not that we are recent acquaintances. He is like a son to us," asserted Ruma. Calling his name was an indication that Ruma was not going to be buffaloed. She was then an equal adversary.

However, Shamol was very angry. He had waited the entire afternoon boiling inside to spit the venom out after Sanjay left.

"I don't care what the boy loves; he is not my grandson. Moreover, Sanjay is not my son. I will have to go again and buy some *hilsa*. You know how expensive it has become these days and you serve it to people we see once in two months," Shamol sat down breathing heavily.

"And how often do we see Samrat?" asked Ruma.

Shamol suddenly felt very cold. He could feel the innumerable bumps forming on his forearms, screaming for attention. He had no answer.

"Let Samrat live his life, he is in America, raising a son, like we did; Let him go, we have a life to live and look forward to each day. Why don't you accept Sanjay's proposal?" Ruma pleaded.

Shamol lifted his bony but erect frame, put on his *Kurta*, grabbed a stick and bolted out of the house like a boisterous warrior. He headed straight to the fish market.

Tuesday Morning

"Where are Latika and my grandson?" asked Shamol, perplexed to see only Samrat standing with a small suitcase and a handbag at the door.

It was five AM and his flight had landed on time. Outside, the sky was dark and the streets were quiet.

Samrat looked bone-tired, probably due to the long flight. He had a round face, double chin, big eyes and thick eyebrows. His hair density had thinned considerably and the crown was conspicuous. Loose flesh that hung clumsily over his belt swayed as he walked.

Without any response or explanation, Samrat walked to and bowed before Ruma who was sitting at the dining table. She rose and hugged her son.

"Samrat, where is Latika and Arnav?" Shamol repeated. The irritation in his tone, laced with apprehension, was not lost.

"They did not come. Latika could not get leave from her work," Samrat said weakly as he adjusted his heavy frame on the relatively smaller chair.

"But this is Christmas time. I believe that the whole of America is shut down for celebration. She must complain to her seniors…maybe… file a suit," said Shamol, enraged and serious.

"Arnav appears quite big in the last photos that you had sent us," smiled Ruma, trying to change the topic.

"You come after two years without our only grandchild," said Shamol dejectedly to no one in particular. His elaborate plans to entertain his grandson, to take him for long walks in the neighbourhood park, to pamper him lavishly, crashed like a hit fighter plane spiraling down in a free fall.

"You must be very tired; Shoma has made your room spic and span. Get some rest, we have a lot of time to share" said Ruma as she stood up.

Samrat slept through lunch. Shamol checked on his beloved son a couple of times to make sure he was comfortable and adequately covered with a soft blanket. *'Samrat has a propensity to fall sick whenever he visits his country, the dust and pollution must be the culprit'*, Shamol nodded to himself. *And you always come during winters,* he sighed.

The old couple ate a quick silent lunch and retired to their own activities. Shamol went back to his morning incomplete crossword and Ruma to her garden to tend a few pots and admire her lovely yellow dahlias.

"Are you feeling fresh now?" Shamol wondered aloud. He took delight in the envious expressions elicited by some of his neighbours or colleagues whenever they heard of Samrat's prosperity. He was happy that his son was doing well in a faraway land. On the other hand, one corner of his heart longed for his son to return, for him to munificently spoil his only grandchild and for his dear wife to relax by giving the household responsibility to their daughter-in-law. The latter voice was indisputably louder.

"Ruma, give him some more rice, he appeared so fatigued and drained in the morning. He skipped lunch too," smiled Shamol at Samrat. They were seated for dinner.

"I brought fresh *Hilsa* for you yesterday. Fresh. Your mother has really prepared it well. The gravy is yummy," Shamol was unstoppable.

"This fish has too many bones," complained Samrat without looking up from his plate. He was laboriously trying to separate a tiny bone from the soft flesh with his pudgy fingers near to his eyes as if he were admiring an uncut diamond through a magnifying piece.

"You have thinned down from the last time you were here. I know you gorge on unhealthy junk food in America. Try to strengthen your immune system while you are here. You will not get this preparation in America. Ruma, Give him another piece," ordered Shamol adoringly.

"No baba, I don't want another. Even this is taking ages to finish," said Samrat as he gently placed a bone on the edge of his plate.

"I think you have gained some weight, particularly the stomach region," said Ruma.

Shamol did not press further. He gave a nervous glance to Ruma who was peering at him.

Wednesday Morning

"Don't fight! I will give equally to both of you. This is not the last time you are having hilsa," scolded Ruma.

She was feeding them together, a regular affair on Sundays. Samrat would accompany his father to the fish market and Sanjay made it a point to invite himself for lunch.

"You always give him the bigger piece. I go with baba to the fish market and why does he get a bigger piece? I do not like him. I don't want to play with him," Samrat wailed.

Sanjay began grinning and opened his mouth to show the big morsel, which infuriated Samrat further. He howled more.

"Don't cry Samrat, you can have my piece too," offered Shamol who could not contain himself any longer.

"No, I want the piece Ma gave to Sanjay" Samrat cried as he climbed to his father's lap.

"Why don't you take care and give them equally?" said Shamol as he wiped his son's tears.

"Come on Shamol; they are kids and you also don't have to act like one," pointed Ruma. "Samrat is being rude and ill-mannered and you must not back him."

Shamol woke up with a start. He was sweating and felt uneasy in his chest. No pain - but a strange anxiety, an inexplicable dread. He switched on the lamp on his side and looked at Ruma who was blissfully unaware. It was four in the morning.

"I have something very important to tell you" started Samrat. He had gone for a walk in the morning and looked fresh. Samrat had been unforthcoming since arrival as if he was entangled in some internal conflict. His old Parents, as always, provided him with ample space and time to unwind.

The family was seated at their usual place in the garden for breakfast. Shamol looked up from above his newspaper.

"I want to take care and be with both of you," said Samrat looking from one to another. He spoke with a dubious sincerity as if he had practiced the line to perfection.

Ruma was skeptical and Shamol joyous.

"Latika and I have decided that both of you should come and stay with us forever in America," said Samrat ardently as if his parents were dying for that offer.

"That's good," said Shamol. His son was not keen on returning, but that is fine, he thought. Ruma often reminded him without mincing words that he was living in denial. Somewhere deep down he had been prepared.

"I am planning to start a venture with an American partner and would need around half a million dollars to be an equal shareholder. We have worked out the project and hope to roll it by the middle of next year," continued Samrat.

Samrat hesitated a moment and said with some conviction "I need that money, baba."

"But I don't have any Samrat and don't think that at my age of seventy anybody would be interested in loaning it to me. My days are over Samrat," he said gently. He was looking at his wife as he spoke.

He turned to his son and smiled. "In fact I was going to ask you to send some more money regularly as things are becoming expensive by the day and you have not sent any money for the past six months".

Ruma had dropped her knitting and was all ears for the *tete-a-tete.*

"That's what I am saying, we could sell this house and all live together in America. You can be with your grandson. In fact I have talked to some agents and they say your house can easily fetch more than half a million," said Samrat, looking from one to another, the urgency and uneasiness in his tone was out in the open.

The words hit Shamol like lightening. . He.... suddenly felt... enervated.... lifeless. His morning chest pain resurfaced while his stomach churned below the navel. His eyes glistened with a layer of tears that struggled to form a drop against his will.

Samrat noticed his father's gloomy appearance but then it was not going to be easy, he thought.

Shamol turned slowly, looked at his wife's sad eyes and fell in love with her, yet again. He knew exactly what those beautiful eyes were saying.

He let out a deep sigh, wiped his tears with the edge of his white *kurta* without any sign of resistance or embarrassment.

He spoke deliberately and slowly.

"Samrat, in the morning, your mother and I were having a chat and we decided to lease your room on rent to Sanjay and his family. He has been pestering your mother for years and I, hopeful of your return one day, was not agreeing to it. You know how much he loves your mother," Shamolda spoke confidently as if sure of himself.

"You can stay in the guest room when you visit us for a week or fortnight," said Shamol neatly folding the newspaper. He looked straight into his son's eyes.

Samrat was at a loss for words. He had expected some resistance, dilly-dallying and persuasion but not outright rejection. He scrambled for an opening to say something.

It was his turn to hide his tears.

"But…but…why Sanjay…?" he had never liked Sanjay.

"Oh! I love that boy, what is his name? Yes! Shujit. The child just loves *Hilsa,*" concluded Shamol softly to himself

Time stopped…. and Ruma felt one with Shamol…. yet again.

♡

The Stolen Pride

Monday: 0715 hrs.

"I cannot find my Physics book!" Ronit shouted nervously. He had overturned his room as he searched frantically but the book remained elusive.

"It's time. The bus will be at the stop in five minutes," Lisa yelled from outside his room.

"Mama…. I cannot find my Physics book," he cried out again. Thin lines of sweat sprouted on his forehead and above his lips.

Lisa barged in with his Lunch box in her hand. She was in her night pajamas and a loose T-shirt. Her long hair was loosely tied in a bun and a pair of silver rings dangled from the helix of her ear on both sides; the earlobe flaunted a diamond dangler.

"Your room is in a sheer mess. Where do I start? Its madness," Lisa snubbed. She raised her arms and let it drop to firmly clasp her waist as she surveyed the clutter.

"Here! No! No! It's biology. Both are of exactly the same size…right?" she fumbled with a pile of books in front of her.

"The Physics one has a pink chequered hard cover," said Ronit who was on the floor with a torch light, focusing it under his bed.

"Don't mess up your uniform. We don't have time for all this," frowned Lisa

"You will miss School if we delay any further."

"But I have a Physics class today and Mr. Ved makes it a point to ascertain that each student has his book opened in front of him. He is very strict," lamented Ronit as he stood up. He was on the verge of tears. Ronit looked dapper with a clean uniform, well-groomed hair, socks that touched his knees and a pair of shining shoes. He was skinny with thick brows, big eyes, thin lips and a sparse hair growth above his lips. He was twelve and hated Physics, in fact he disliked studies altogether but as is the system – cultural or societal, the hapless students have limited say. Be safe with the herd or perish, that is the mantra.

"How many times have I told you to arrange your bag before going to bed? You are always short of time in the morning. These things should have been taken care of yesterday. God! When will you grow up?" lamented Lisa, as if that would solve the crisis at hand.

Ronit stood transfixed like a volcano, fighting hard to quell the uneasiness churning in his stomach and the tears fighting to break free. Lisa softened on sensing his misery.

"Don't worry, Ronit," urged Lisa as her son wiped the layer of dust from his knees and elbows. "I will arrange the room and I am sure we will find the book,"

"But…"

"No buts, you cannot miss school for a book," said Lisa sternly. "You know how particular your dad is in these matters. He will be very angry that you lost your book and missed school for that."

The sudden inflection brought the discussion to an abrupt denouement. Dad's stern demeanour instantly came alive on his mind's screen, automatically stimulating him into action. Lisa picked the heavy school bag and handed it to her son. With a worried expression, Ronit pushed the tiffin box inside and walked out of the room.

Monday: 1105 hrs.

"Why is your book not opened?" asked Mr. Ved grimly. He wore a loose cream shirt with straight brown trousers. Mr. Ved was around six feet with a big nose and a thin moustache that was curled up at the ends. Students of the school had nicknamed him 'Anti-Hero' as handsome looks were complemented with an inclination to dress immaculately. His serious and no nonsense approach earned his sobriquet the unwanted prefix.

Ronit stood with his head bowed.

"Where is your Physics book, Ronit?" a noticeable impatience crept into his tone.

Ronit looked up. Mr. Ved, with the rest of the class, was intently gazing at the isolated and nervous child. "I...I...forgot," he was barely audible.

"What?" Mr. Ved frowned, "You forgot?" he sneered.

Ronit was motionless, lifeless like an Egyptian mummy.

"How many times do I have to remind you all that I want the book every time in my class?" bellowed Mr. Ved at the class. "Ronit thinks it's not serious, he believes Mr. Ved would not notice, that Mr. Ved is stupid to always insist for the book," he stomped on the aisle, peering at the students as he crossed them.

"Do you think I am a fool?" he roared at the class.

No one said anything.

"Do you?" he shouted again.

"No sir," immediately came a nervous chorus.

"No Sir. You are smart but I don't understand Physics," a voice came alive inside Ronit.

"Do I ever forget to bring the book to the class?" he wondered aloud.

'*You have a locker here. You don't have to carry books behind your back every day,*' Ronit wanted to say.

"I would like to have a word with your father regarding this…this misdemeanor," Mr. Ved halted near Ronit.

Ronit's knees went weak and his face drained of colour as if life had been sucked out of it. He wanted to implore Mr. Ved to keep his dad out of this matter. He longed to say that he had made a sincere effort to locate the book but his search had been futile; that he will surely find the book and get it for the next class, but no words came out of his mouth.

"Is that clear?" asked Mr. Ved patronizingly into his ear, the distance between them was almost negligible.

"I…I…will bring it next time," he stammered.

Mr. Ved walked to the dais and sat behind his wooden desk. "Ronit, go and stand outside the classroom," he ordered as he opened his Physics book.

Monday: 1445 hrs.

"That is my book! Hey look! Outside. Out of the window," Amar, the plum cheeked and chubby boy was animated. He was frantically pointing to an object outside the window. An opened crumpled book lay on the ground, out in the open.

He pulled the spectacled Rama, who was sharpening his pencil.

"Your book?" squinted Rama, looking out of the window.

Couple of more classmates joined the commotion, straining their neck for a better view. One of them pushed himself upon frail Rama's bony shoulders for support.

"It's my Physics book!" cried Amar apprehensively, finally recognizing it fully.

"How did it go outside? Amar's physics book can fly," someone shouted.

"Yes! How did it go outside the window?" asked Amar agitated. He was getting jittery.

"Alas! My books cannot fly," pretentiously sobbed Yash, the mischievous chap, who relished bullying his friends.

"Even mine cannot fly," his cronies sang and giggled.

Some more students joined in to form several circular layers with Amar, John and Rama racking their grey cells at the centre.

"Is your name written on it?" wondered John, a conscientious, serious and no-nonsense guy, the blue-eyed boy of the class teacher. He was the class monitor. He pushed aside his mates, who were clinging to the metal lattice, to get another view of the unfortunate book.

"Yes, of course. On the first page," said Amar with a nervous excitement.

"I will go out and bring the book. Amar, you come with me," commanded John.

No one noticed the quiet guy seated one row behind, who listened attentively to the confusion. After several aborted attempts during the day, he could snatch the exact moment, hidden from everyone, to push the thick book through the metal grid in one swift motion. He was praying fervently to prevent Amar from noticing his missing book. *'Another fifteen minutes'* he had urged God. Last hour of the day, a free one without any teacher, was his best chance, he had told himself.

He had another day to create a book for himself.

Monday: 2105 hrs.

"How are your studies?" asked Mr. Sanjeev Shaw gravelly. His deep voice did not fail to instill anxiety in Ronit.

"Ok," said Ronit. *'I cannot find my Physics book.'*

"Hmmm," he said, taking a swig from his drink.

Ronit hated it when occasionally, his father, after a couple of drinks, would suddenly remember his elder son and lavishly pour his cynical attention. Ronit began nibbling at the Roti, his appetite awry while his father sat with his glass, his undivided attention focused on Ronit. Seated beside him, Sombit, his brother, three years younger, ate enthusiastically, unconcerned by the turbulence ripping Ronit apart.

Sanjeev viewed himself as a principled and an upright man who considered it apt to frequently lecture his son on morality or the correct way of life.

"When I was your age, I used to wake up at five in the morning and walk all the way to school," he began predictably. "Look at you…you are always exhausted and fatigued."

Ronit was uninterested. His opinion would be interpreted as blatant argument or disrespect.

"Things are becoming very expensive these days; school fees, books, vegetables. You better do well in studies and grow up fast to be on your own," Sanjeev stared wide-eyed at Ronit. His forehead was moulded into a permanent frown.

'The new book will cost only five hundred rupees.' 'What! Five hundred rupees! How could you lose such an expensive book?'

'As if it were fine to lose anything cheap,' the voice would not stop.

Ronit wished his father to be expressive of his love, delicate and approachable. He yearned to share his world with his father; longed for his guidance whenever he would be stuck in his studies, but the bond was slowly getting strained, rusty and weak with neglect. Sanjeev was steadily becoming a slave to his drinks. Listening to his son was not his idea of an evening well spent.

'What about alcohol? You do not complain about its price. As if it is very cheap. Why don't you stop drinking,' mused Ronit. 'He would kill me if I asked him to buy a new Physics book.'

Monday: 2215 hrs.

"I could not find the book in your room," said Lisa. The brothers shared a common room. Sombit was busy in his area of the room.

"I found it in School," said Ronit hastily to bury the issue. He did not want the matter to leak out of the room.

"Be careful with your stuff in School. Someone could have taken it," advised Lisa.

"Why is Baba always serious?" asked Ronit.

"He is a little worried about his work. He will be fine. He loves you a lot," stressed Lisa

"If he is worried, why does he drink every day?" asked Ronit earnestly.

"It's late, dear. You have School tomorrow. Good night," Lisa smiled. She wished her children would stop growing. At least she would be spared of all the difficult questions.

'The next Physics class is on Wednesday,' Ronit stared into darkness, wide-awake.

Tuesday: 1500 hrs.

His classmates were on alert during the day, overcautious after the 'flying book' episode of the day before and they diligently guarded their bags. As the school had broken for the day, ten minutes after the confusion, everyone tacitly concurred to let the matter subside without bringing it to the class teacher's notice. No one had lost anything after all.

'None would have brought their Physics book today. It's Tuesday. So don't attempt any indiscretion,' a voice cautioned him. Ronit was the last person to leave the classroom as he embarked on a lonely and depressed walk to the waiting bus. Since morning, his restless mind had devoted every breath to assemble a book like a jigsaw puzzle but it remained bereft of any concrete solution.

A shiver ran down his spine as he visualized himself amidst the draconian Principle and his nervous father, contemplating retributive punishment to instill some morality. Theft was a serious charge that cannot be overlooked, they would agree with unprecedented fury in their eyes.

'I am sorry for stealing, but I am not very keen on studies. I want to play Badminton. I want to be a Professional sportsman. The coach says I can rise to international standard through focused training.'

His throat was parched. He took a gulp of warm water from his bottle.

Confronting his father to confess the loss of Physics book was unimaginable. His father would neither raise his hand nor shun him forever or quit loving him in his strange ways. But verbal bashing on responsibility and organization would be meted out, as if he were filth, and a constant reminder of his carelessness would be played out for days. The evening ordeal at the dining table would become unbearable. The incident could be pulled out from the archives of memory at random to score a point or highlight some other weakness.

Requesting his beloved mother for a new book, concealed from her husband was unthinkable. Even if she agreed, she might, unintentionally, blurt it out at a later date to invite his wrath.

'How could he loose such a thick book? It is unacceptable,' muttered Ronit to himself, imitating his father.

'Only few hours are left to find the blessed book,' reminded Ronit while boarding the bus.

Tuesday: 2015hrs.

"I am going to Aparna's house," said Ronit. He wore a navy blue slacks with blue and white checkered half shirt that hung loosely over his thin frame. His right hand firmly clasped two textbooks.

Aparna was a classmate who lived in the neighbourhood.

"It's late! Why?" Lisa asked as she applied pink water colour on Sombit's drawing book.

'Because I have no other option!'

"We have a biology test tomorrow. I thought we could ask questions to each other and revise. It would be faster," said Ronit.

"You should have gone a little earlier. This is not the time to knock at someone's door." Lisa was irritated and perplexed.

"It will not take long, just half an hour. Please," Ronit was desperate.

"How do you know she needs a companion to revise?" frowned his mother.

Ronit waited for her mother to make up her mind.

"Don't be long," asserted Lisa.

Ronit nodded, turned around and vanished from her sight before his mother could come up with something or decided to change her mind.

"Hello Aunty," Ronit smiled. It took him five minutes of brisk walk to reach Aparna's apartment.

"Ronit?" asked Mrs. Roy, a little surprised. "Don't you have a biology test tomorrow?"

"Yes Aunty," said Ronit eagerly. "I have some doubts in chapter six. I think Aparna can definitely throw some light," said Ronit, scratching his head. He knew Mrs. Roy would not be very keen to allow group revision.

"Now?" Mrs. Roy was irritated as expected.

Ronit stared at his sandals. It was not going to be effortless. He knew that.

"You may not be serious about the exam, but Aparna is," Mrs. Roy was fixed at the entrance. "You should have cleared your doubts earlier, not a few hours before the exam," scolded Mrs. Roy as she adjusted her blue cotton sari.

"But it's only a class test," Ronit immediately regretted the casual sentence.

"A test is a test, however insignificant!" Mrs. Roy glared. "Your generation needs serious bashing," she declared.

"Please Aunty! I will not take long, not more than half an hour," pleaded Ronit. Time was steadily slipping away and Mrs. Roy here was determined to ruin his evening, thought Ronit. At this rate, whatever biology he had studied would be wiped clean.

"This is the last time you are allowed for doubts a day before the exam. That's not how Aparna manages her studies," came the final warning.

"Thank you Aunty," said Ronit as he bent to squeeze past Mrs. Roy.

Aparna was short with big eyes on a small round face that appeared disproportionate or cute depending on an individual's perspective. Her long black hair was bunched into two distinct plaits that extended halfway down her back. At first impression, to an untrained eye, she might come across as timid or coy, an opinion that changed swiftly after the first interaction. Aparna was feisty, intelligent and a girl with a mind of her own.

"Hi," smiled Ronit.

"Hello," she smiled back.

"So, are you ready for the exam tomorrow? Last month Mrs. D'Souza had set a tough paper. I hope she remembers that," said Ronit as he pulled a chair to join Aparna opposite her, at her study table.

"I have revised twice," said Aparna as she toyed with a pen between her teeth.

"Twice! Wow! Great!" he exclaimed.

"How did my mother allow you inside?" Aparna squinted.

"Oh! It was tough. You know your mother," grinned Ronit. "And you also know me," he tugged at his collar proudly. "I have been given thirty minutes. I have some doubts in chapter six,"

"Doubts? Chapter six? It's the easiest one!" ridiculed Aparna.

Tuesday: 2115 hrs.

"Thanks for clearing the doubts. Mrs. D'Souza can never explain so clearly. Do you take tuitions?" asked Ronit, sitting straight.

"No tuition. Whenever I am stuck, I ask my Dad. He dwells on it until I genuinely comprehend it. He says one has to have one's fundamentals strong," she beamed proudly.

'I wish…my dad…' Ronit exhaled.

"I shall take your leave before Aunty comes with a reminder," Ronit pushed the plastic chair and got up.

"She has already checked twice," snickered Aparna.

"Bye Aunty," said Ronit as Mrs. Roy slammed the door behind him.

Neither Aparna nor her mother noticed the addition of a thick book in Ronit's hand as he walked past them on his way out.

Tuesday: 2120 hrs.

"Apu," Mr. Rana Roy stood at the entrance to his daughter's room. He was short like Aparna, stout with a chubby face and a short neck. He walked straight with a conspicuous potbelly that shook violently whenever he guffawed. He was perky and jovial in nature.

"A moment Dad," said Aparna from under the table.

"What is the matter dear?" Rana asked indifferently.

"I have a physics class tomorrow," she said.

"So?"

"I wanted to pack my bag for tomorrow but cannot find the Physics book," she said as she stood up to face him. "It has been lying on this table since yesterday," she said worryingly.

"Did you check the shelf over there?" he asked.

"I did. I saw it this evening on this table," she said with one hand on the table and another on her hip.

"Are you sure?"

"Yes Dad"

"I saw it right here," she pointed to the exact spot.

"Then where did it go?" Rana was scratching his dry chin.

"Mr. Ved would kill me without the book," Aparna's eyes shined with a layer of moistness.

"It must be here somewhere," he encouraged.

"I have searched everywhere, Dad. I have been searching since Ronit left. You don't know Mr. Ved," she fidgeted.

"How can a book vanish from the table?" he sat on the chair opposite Aparna's.

"I saw Ronit taking notes on top of my book on a plain paper," she frowned. "Yes, he was!" she jumped. "So, it was here. I told you."

"I believe you darling," said Rana, staring at the room for any clue to the lost book.

"Has Ronit taken it by mistake, along with his biology book?" wondered Aparna aloud.

"But that's a heavy book to carry inadvertently. Your Physics book is not an advertisement flyer that will get lost between books," he recalled, scratching his fat cheek.

Aparna nodded. She was bereft of any more ideas.

"Did he lift it deliberately?" Mr. Roy looked straight at his daughter. His gaze pierced her eyes, searching for any clue.

"But why would he?" Aparna was bewildered.

"I don't know," said Rana as he stared at the spotless wooden desk. His daughter was fastidious to a fault and she always knew exactly where she kept her things. And that Ronit came across as clumsy, untidy and insincere.

"Let's go," he commanded.

Tuesday: 2145 hrs.

"Hello. I am Mr. Roy, Aparna's father," he said to answer Lisa's confused and apprehensive expression.

"Aha! Aparna," she smiled as she noticed the tentative little girl beside her father.

"I know it's a little late and I would not have called if it were unimportant. Can we come in for a minute?" asked Mr. Roy without divulging any emotions.

"Sure. Sure," nodded Lisa. "Please come inside."

"This is Mr. Roy. My husband," said Lisa, introducing the two males. "Please sit."

Sanjeev waved from his seat.

"Would you like a drink?" asked Sanjeev, lowering the TV volume.

"No, thank you. I don't drink," said Rana uncomfortably.

"I enjoy a couple of drinks to unwind before retiring for the day," grinned Sanjeev like a child displaying his favourite toy and took a sip from his glass.

Aparna scanned the room but Ronit was not in sight. She wanted the ordeal to be over at the earliest. What if her book was lying in some corner of her room? She quivered at the thought.

But her father had already pressed the trigger.

"Well...I don't know how to put it..." began Rana uncertainly. The Shaw's looked at each other and then fixed their gaze on Mr. Roy who seemed restive.

"Any problem?" asked Sanjeev seriously.

Mr. Roy took a deep breath, straightened himself and said, "Well, my daughter's Physics book is missing and since Ronit was at our place to discuss biology, I was wondering if he might have unknowingly carried it back with him. You see, the book was on the very table they used."

"We have a Physics class tomorrow and everyone must bring their book," said Aparna worryingly to support her father and justify their presence at an unholy hour.

"How can he carry the book by mistake, even if it's a small book?" Sanjeev was attentive.

"Just to check with him," said Mr. Roy hurriedly. "We looked everywhere in Aparna's room but could not trace it."

"Ronit!" Sanjeev yelled menacingly.

Ronit emerged instantly as if he was on his way to see them. His face had lost colour and his thumb ceaselessly chafed against his fingers while his heart fluttered rapidly. He stood beside his mother, awaiting the next move.

'So soon! As if Aparna and his father rushed after me.'

"Did you go to Aparna's house in the evening?" Sanjeev wanted to be in control.

'God! You would have known if you took a little interest in your son. Stop it Ronit! This is a grim situation that can easily go out of hand. Be cool.'

"Yes," he said.

"For what?" Sanjeev was getting restless.

"To study biology. We have a test tomorrow. I had some doubts," said Ronit calmly, his fingers feeling one another.

"Doubts? You don't have to go anywhere to clear your doubts. You should come straight to me," said Sanjeev forcefully.

"It's Ok. He can come anytime to discuss. That's not the issue here," intervened Mr. Roy, peeved at the sudden shift from his central enquiry.

"I know that. He is my son and I must know why and where he goes," Sanjeev was reluctant to relinquish control.

"Ronit, by mistake, did you bring Aparna's Physics book?" continued Rana ignoring Sanjeev. He endeavoured to be genial, although he would have preferred to hit Ronit's room and ransack it violently. Ronit's reply did not matter to him since he believed that it was impossible or impractical to erroneously carry the book.

"Aparna's book?" Ronit feigned. The response was thoroughly rehearsed, as if he were expecting them at his door anytime.

"Her book has been missing since you left," said Mr. Roy. The friendly tone was gradually fading away.

"No, I did not. I have my own book. I just packed it for tomorrow," said Ronit innocently.

An eerie silence ensued as Mr. Roy and the rest kept staring at Ronit. The discerning Mr. Roy could feel some disquiet in Ronit, a pretense, and a forced calmness that was oblivious to his father but not his mother.

"Can I see your Physics book?" Aparna asked, handing a lifeline to her father.

"What?" Sanjeev erupted

Lisa twitched her lips to silence Sanjeev who was ready for another protest.

"Yes, why not?" concurred Ronit immediately and that confused his Parents and particularly Mr. Roy.

"Go and bring your book," Lisa urged her son.

Sanjeev excused himself to make another drink.

Ronit was back in a jiffy. He carried the book at chest height, gently embracing it as if unwilling to part with it.

"The cover looks exactly like mine," she muttered. "I had underlined important paragraphs with pencil in almost all chapters. Can I have a look?" Aparna rose and extended her arm.

"Sure," Ronit had no choice.

Sanjeev was back in his seat. The unfolding drama was making him sick and furious. 'If it wasn't for Lisa, I would have crushed this nonsense much earlier,' he declared to himself.

Sitting beside her father, who was anxious but alert, Aparna carefully took the book on her lap. The book felt so much like hers.

Neat pages devoid of any markings stared at her as she commenced a meticulous scanning of the initial pages. Hope turned into despair as she skimmed through the whole book. She could not trace a single dot of pencil charcoal. She flipped back and forth several times without really looking at the book.

"I…. I… had marked the important chapters with pencil," she looked up with a pair of moist eyes at her father. In her heart, she knew that the book she held was hers without the markings. She wanted to go home and cry.

"I do not mark my books," pointed Ronit immediately.

"Let's go," Mr. Roy rose without warning. He tugged at Aparna who was still holding the book to her chest. He mumbled an inaudible apology to Lisa, refrained from acknowledging Sanjeev, irritatingly pushed Aparna to hurry and headed towards the exit. Aparna dropped the book on the sofa and followed her father.

Tuesday: 2230 hrs.

"What insolence!" barked Sanjeev as Lisa closed the door. "They were blatantly accusing our son of theft. Did you see that?"

"I know," she had no option but to agree though she was struggling with her own doubts. She sat beside her husband.

"And you," he turned his attention to his son who was fixed near his book. Ronit knew the final assault was inescapable. "No one can point a finger at my son. My son," he shouted, the emotions that were restrained to avoid a social faux pa, flowed freely like waterfall, hitting all in its way.

"If you want, I will buy you ten books, but I would not tolerate anyone coming to my house and blatantly charging my son with theft. Do you get that?" he asked sternly.

Ronit nodded meekly.

"I don't know what he is learning in School," he frowned, turning to his wife. "And that impudent girl has the nerve to ask for the book. I felt like throwing them out of the house. I don't want you to go to her house ever," he said, maintaining the stony face.

Ronit nodded.

"Ronit, eat your dinner and hit the bed. You have school tomorrow," said Lisa, seizing on the brief silence.

Ronit stood up, book in his hand and slowly walked out of the living room. He did not notice that his mother was not able to take her eyes off the blue chequered hardcover Physics book from the moment he had brought it in.

Tuesday: 2330 hrs.

Lisa turned off the lights without wishing 'good night' to the kids. Ronit lay fully awake. He stared at the ceiling as the events of the evening unfurled randomly. *Ronit had run all the way from Aparna's house, covering the stretch in a minute. 'Aparna Roy' was the first words that he erased. He continued to rub vigorously unmindful of the pain that gripped his arms, wrist and brows. He expunged all underlines, short notes and any inadvertent pencil marks. Sweating profusely, he flipped the book four times and strained his eyes to scan every single page to confirm.*

It was as if he was sure that the bell would ring any second.

Rest of the Days

The Physics book or any strand of the incident was never repeated or even accidentally mentioned in that household. Things returned to normal, as it always does with time.

Sanjeev suspected that his son was guilty of the misdemeanor, but then if he probed further and forced Ronit to relent, it would be a stain on his principles and style of upbringing, exposing him to direct line of fire. It would be a burden that he was incapable of carrying. As the adage goes, some things are best buried, he told himself.

Lisa knew her son had stolen the book, but could not muster the courage to confront him. She also knew that it would break Sanjeev's heart to face the truth. It was not proved, she reasoned. What if it becomes a habit? The prospect choked her. She vowed to take more interest in Ronit's activities.

Ronit never met Aparna again. *'Her father must have ordered her to stay away from me'.* She knew it was her book, the moment she touched it, Ronit could see it in her eyes. He would look straight ahead whenever he crossed her balcony. *'I would not be able to face her…look her in the eye.'* A good friend was lost forever, but then he was only twelve…he would have many more, he assured himself.

His pride was intact, his honour was untouched…and most importantly he was still the good son, who cannot err…. like his father…who never erred.

When a wrongdoing is extremely shameful or regretful, it is pushed far deep into a secret vault in our mind where, even we are forbidden access to it. And we live with total conviction that it never happened.

When his father, his hero, joined him for dinner, he could still look into his father's eyes without shame…and with pride.

The Mirage

"Hello son! Is anyone home, your Dad? Mom?" smiled Sher Singh.

"Why?" looking up, the belligerent kid frowned, his hands placed firmly on his hips. He squinted to examine Sher Singh like a tiger measuring his prey before totally committing to the kill.

"I have something important for them," Sher Singh smiled again.

"You can tell me," the kid persisted

"You will not understand son; how old are you? Seven? Eight?" he contemplated, rolling his eyeballs.

"I am not sure whether your parents would comprehend either," he muttered under his breath. "Why don't you call your father? Tell him an uncle would like to talk to him for five minutes," smiled Sher Singh

"He is sleeping," said the kid coming closer, his twisted posture unchanged.

"Now! It's eleven," said Sher Singh incredulously as if the sun had risen from the wrong direction. He, tuned to his military background, considered such languidness a crime. It was unthinkable.

The kid grimaced as if bewildered. His interest was waning off. "It's Sunday today; no office," he explained, as if it were his father's right to rise at noon on Sundays.

"Who are you talking to Vicky?" "Yes?" Mrs. Khurana came to the door and stood behind her son with an anxious expression, relieving Sher Singh of the nightmare.

"Hello Mam," said Sher pleasantly. "Here, Please take this; it's for you," he took out a sheet from his file.

Mrs. Khurana gave a cursory glance and looked up, fishing for some clarity. Her chest was wrapped with a big towel to camouflage her single piece nighty.

"What is it? Are you selling something? We are not interested," she said firmly, taking a step back.

"No Mam," Sher Singh replied calmly.

"Then is it some sort of 'get rich quick scheme?' MLM?" frowned Mrs. Khurana.

"No…No," came the quick reply.

"Some vacation thing?" her brain was on an overdrive.

"No! No! No! Nothing like that" panicked Sher Singh sensing the aversion and distrust. "I am working for an NGO; My Planet Our Home; see…here," pointed Sher to the header on the form that dangled loosely between Mrs. Khurana's fingers, "and we spread awareness on several subjects that concern our beautiful planet, man-made pits into which our planet is slipping fast, unless we wake up and take stock of the situation to reverse the tide" paused Sher Singh for effect.

Mrs. Khurana stared blankly, unable to comprehend a word. She was getting edgy. It was Sunday and things were lazily behind schedule. Saving the planet did not feature in the mental list that she had chalked out in the morning for the day.

"If you allow me a minute, simply put," continued Sher Singh hurriedly, sensing the unenthusiastic body language, "we deal with topics such as global warming, potable water consumption, tree plantations for greener colonies, taking on the government on green clearances for urban project, etc., issues that should be a concern for   any responsible person in this era of prolific urbanization and total dependence on fossil fuel."

"So?" Mrs. Khurana was getting impatient. It was still Latin to her.

"How much water does your family consume every day?" asked Sher Singh, coming to the point.

"How do I know?" asked Mrs. Khurana, flabbergasted. "We have never measured that. And why should we? We are diligently paying our water bills."

"Maybe your husband would have a better idea," suggested Sher, unable to break through. .

"Husband?" mocked Mrs. Khurana; "I would be surprised if, amidst several overhead tank on the terrace, belonging to all the families in this building, he could locate ours. Anyway he is sleeping."

"That is exactly why I am here," said Sher emphatically. "Most of us are totally unaware of how much water we consume and how by minor tweaks in our daily habits, we can actually save a substantial quantity which can be made available to millions of impoverished families who are without potable water, in our country and globally."

He hoped the young lady would invite her inside and offer some water. His leg, from standing at a place, had begun to ache.

Sher Singh was sixty-six, over six feet and straight as a rod. Every morning, he would religiously oil his thick hair; that is the secret of my dense mane, he would declare proudly when asked by his mostly bald peers. More than forty years in the army manifested as a disciplined soldier who rose with the Sun at five and loved his exercise, an attribute that remains the privilege of a determined few. He vehemently advocated being fit as the doorway to a healthy mind and happiness, a claim none could refute.

"Mam, as you know, water is vital for our survival, an element without which we stand absolutely no chance. But the commodity is becoming scarcer each single day. World over, countries are pushing its citizens through regulation and awareness to save water, in fact Germany is encouraging its citizens to bring down an individual's personal water needs to 100 liters per person per day. The Indian average among urban population varies between 240 liters to 600 liters per person per day," explained Sher patiently, forsaking any chance of being offered some water.

Mrs. Khurana was explicitly agitated and scouting for an opening to call off the dull conversation but refrained from being overtly blunt or rude out of sheer respect for an old man.

"Just a little more, Mam. I won't take much of your important time. Please take this poster; it depicts diverse ways to save water in our everyday activities such as shaving, bathing, cleaning, use of water saving commodes, etc. It is very informative and you can paste it at a common area such as on the fridge or near your bathroom mirror. Your eyes would unavoidably catch the poster whenever you cross or open your fridge and the idea to save water would remain alive," suggested Sher confidently.

"And on this page you can fill in approximate figures to record the family's daily use. If filled diligently over a period, it will give you a comprehensive idea about your water consumption; whether it's on the rise, maintaining, etc. Needless to say, it will reflect on your water bills and more importantly you would do your bit for your planet," he finished just before Mrs. Khurana slammed the door. She was left with no other option.

Sher Singh took a moment to enter some details such as house no., etc. of the Khuranas into his diary before stepping out on the road. Mrs. Khurana had been generously patient, which was more than he could ask for. Year in and year out, he had come across individuals who had been unabashedly rude, impolite, and cynical.

People are disinclined to service, more so when poked on a Sunday; they are so entangled in the rut for survival and also an abject disregard for any social initiative that lending a tolerant ear for any such purpose for even ten minutes becomes a tedious challenge.

A few months after retiring from the army, Sher Singh had joined an NGO. A hardened community servant, he had always envisioned this path. It gave him a purpose, an engagement and a sense of fulfillment that spurred him to hit the road every morning oblivious to any snub or indifference doled out by the resigned society.

"I will take a break today," he thought feeling feeble and turned towards his house.

"Keep your eyes open, Fateh," yelled Sher Singh into his ears. A thin column of spit stretched from his mouth and dropped on his companion's shoulders.

"I don't think I can make it," coughed Fateh, clutching his abdomen, a thick stream of sputum laced with blood ran down his chin every time he attempted to speak.

"You can!" commanded Sher with conviction. The jugulars on his throat bulged and his face reddened menacingly as he roared to instill some life into his waning buddy.

They could intermittently hear the endless gunfire somewhere at a distance, though Sher was not sure in which direction. The war had consumed them.

Fateh was shot in the ambush, the bullet drilling a gaping hole below his right lung, maybe his liver was punctured; Sher was not sure.

Their regiment was gliding stealthily under forest cover when a sudden fusillade from the opposite direction had stopped them in their tracks. The conflict was over in a matter of minutes. Though the adversaries, a handful of renegade locals with automatics, backed and trained by the military from across the border, were eventually overwhelmed and annihilated, Sher had to turn back with Fateh who needed immediate medical assistance.

He had tightly wrapped a sheet around his buddy's belly after applying betadine soaked in swabs and made Fateh swallow a couple of painkillers from his expedient first aid kit, but the steady loss of blood was alarming.

"There is no hope," a voice in his head had been ranting for some time and he was fighting hard not to succumb to it.

"Let's move; I will carry you," he declared with a start, nudging Fateh, who was resting on a trunk, the shade of the giant tree bestowed a breathing space in their arduous trek to their command position.

It was imperative to reach the camp before nightfall to allow any chance for Fateh's survival; he would not last another day, thought Sher.

"How? You are also shot in the leg!" exclaimed Fateh, laboriously opening his exhausted eyes.

"We have to go!" yelled Sher, pulling his friend's combat shirt with both hands.

"Water!" moaned Fateh.

Sher Singh stared at the ceiling, the ancient fan creaked on every revolution, though at higher ranges it was a faint blip.

"When will it be over," rued Sher aloud; it had been more than thirty years but Fateh's voice, his crestfallen eyes were fresh as the first leaves of spring. Sher glanced at his bedside clock;

four a.m. it said - an hour to go before beginning his morning ritual. He remained on his back with both hands on his chest, palms on top of one another, fingers entwined as if in prayer and waited for his breathing to become normal.

"How is your save water program these days?" asked Deep casually, switching on the TV.

"Same," answered Sher without looking up. His son was on his weekly Sunday visit, which Sher avidly looked forward to, for a chance to be with his adorable grandson. But it was drab that day since Honey did not accompany his parents.

"Deep, please remove the remote from the table," said Simran with a straight face, holding the tray with three cups of tea. Her husband immediately obliged.

Simran collapsed into the couch, her heavy frame causing it to squeak like a squirrel. Sher and Deep reached out for their respective cups.

"Are you taking your BP medicines regularly, Papaji?" Simran was genuinely concerned.

Simran had a deep respect bordering on reverence for her father-in-law, who had a disciplined personality, stately elegance, and was a man of integrity, all of which Simran admired. After her mother-in-law's demise, she had pleaded with Sher to move in with them, a tempting offer when he imagined his grandson's mischievous smile, but each time Sher had politely declined. Years in the army had trained him to survive in the harshest of conditions, and over time he had become a loner. He still had a lot of baggage to shake off.

"How is Honey?" asked Sher to no one in particular.

"There is no fever today, though he is still weak; these days doctors just scribble an antibiotic upon hearing the first symptom and oddly, one does not recover without them. I wonder what we would turn to once these drugs become ineffective," lamented Simran.

"He will be fine; he is a strong boy. Bring him along next time," smiled Sher, taking a sip from his cup.

"Sure, Papaji, goes without saying," Simran concurred.

"Mam, can I speak with you for a minute?" smiled Sher. The lady seemed elegant.

The sonorous voice juxtaposed with a towering personality made the lady flinch. Sher wore a white half shirt that exposed the thick coils of white hair covering his forearms. Plain black trousers with black shoes completed his attire.

Sher, aware of the lady's discomfort, softened the contours of his face. This morning had been frustrating with doors being slammed on him bluntly and some apartments elicited no response upon pressing the doorbell. He was anxious to share his passion – save water, save life.

She seemed to be in her forties, conscious of her diet and workout as revealed by her prominent curves. She exuded an aura of confidence, mindful of her appeal and beauty. She quickly regained her prim composure.

"I am from a NGO – My Planet Our Home," said Sher softly, offering a brochure to the lady.

"Hmmm…so are you looking for some donation?" she said, flipping the pages like a wad of currency notes as if relishing its feel in her hands.

"No, I am not," said Sher earnestly.

In earlier days he would be suspicious on mention of the word 'donation', but over the years, dealing with sundry people, some recalcitrant while others audaciously hostile, had trained him to deal such condescending query with élan.

"Oh!" she said, taken aback. "So, you are selling something," she said, as though she got him.

"No, Mam, if you would just give me a couple of minutes, I shall be quick," Sher was calm.

Sher left satiated. While relishing several homemade cookies and an extra helping of clove tea, he dwelled on each point at length. "What a lady!" he signed. Maria was indulgently forthcoming after an initial bout of cynicism and it turned out to be one of his best interactions. After listening attentively, she lauded Sher for the honorable service he was doing, the struggle he has undertaken and offered to accompany him whenever mutually appropriate, an offer Sher politely declined. Unperturbed, she scribbled her contact details and promised to disturb him on occasions.

"Fateh," barked Sher "don't sleep on me; try to keep those eyes open." He was losing his friend.

Fateh's eyelids opened with a jerk, his eyeballs rolled unconsciously to survey the surroundings and finally settled on Sher. The afternoon sun was intense and the umbrage under the colossal banyan tree was barely comforting. Fateh's throat was parched and he struggled to roll out his tongue to wet his cracked lips.

They were still 24 hours away from the base camp when they marched in normal circumstances. Sher was trying not to think how long it would take under his present condition. Bile rose up his chest and the sour taste made him retch several times.

"Water!" groaned Fateh, barely audible.

Sher reached out for Fateh's bottle lying by his side, removed the lid and placed it carefully on his lips. A few remaining drops rolled out and wetted his mouth. Sher shook the bottle vigorously as if to free the remaining water.

"Wait, Hang On, I have some with me," said Sher and put his bottle to Fateh's eager tongue.

"We have to move now," said Sher, pulling Fateh by his arm.

"You have to save yourself, brother. Please... leave me here. Don't worry. I will be fine. Take this," Fateh was breathless and struggled to regain his strength after each sentence, "this locket with my two sons... give it to them personally and assure them... that you were with their father in his last moments... and that he loves them more than... anything else." Fateh's head dropped due to the exhaustion. He was severely debilitated and had not moved for the past couple of hours, lying against the tree, one hand placed *on his wound while the other, crimson with dried blood, lay on the ground as a lifeless limb. He was almost unconscious.*

Sher knew the inevitable. He knew Fateh was right; that he should move on or else both would perish. He felt the wound on his right calf; the bullet was still inside and although the bleeding had ebbed due to the tourniquet, the severe pain was killing him. He would not be able to carry Fateh for more than a few wayward steps.

"And leave that thing hanging on your shoulder till you are back; I will need some," Fateh winked tediously and let his eyelids drop.

"Sure," said Sher Singh without hesitation.

He woke with a start, gasping for breath; Sweat dripped from his forehead and the back of his head, soaking his cotton pillow. He gulped some water kept on his bedside table and slumped back. Like every morning, he vowed again to repair the ceiling fan; the unmistakable blip was getting louder.

He got up and sat on the edge of his bed, caressing the soft lump below his right knee. The prosthetic leg lay at the far corner of the bed. He reached out for it.

"You wanted to see me, Mr. Verma?" enquired Sher as he opened the squeaky door.

"Oh! Yes! Sher, please come," said Verma politely and rose to aid Sher to a vacant chair on one side of his modest wooden table that was crammed with innumerable untidy files.

Sher brushed aside his hand, indicating his displeasure at the show of sympathy.

Verma stiffened and stood still until Sher was comfortably seated.

"How are you today?" smiled Mr. Verma, sitting down. Mr. Verma oversaw one of the four offices of the NGO.

"All well," said Sher Singh.

"Well, Sher, you have been associated with our organization for close to four years now and you have been stupendous in your work. I must admit that your doggedness in disseminating awareness to save water is unprecedented and inspiring," Mr. Verma paused to light a cigarette, "which brings me to the topic of the day."

Sher Singh stared at his boss, bemused. Being a field man all his life, immaculate and prim meetings made him uneasy. In the last four years, he had entered Mr. Verma's chamber only twice.

"I have one good news and one bad news," offered Verma on noting Sher's predicament. "Which one should I shoot first?" barked Mr. Verma, mimicking a pistol with his fingers, the barrel pointed at Sher.

Sher made no attempt to disclose his choice. He solemnly stared at his boss.

"Let me go for the bad one first," teased Mr. Verma.

"Your services will not be required here anymore," said Mr. Verma.

"Oh!" exclaimed Sher, appalled.

"You are being offered a permanent position in our Mumbai headquarters, a desk job that will no longer be physically taxing. I bet you deserve no less," Mr. Verma thumped his desk excitedly.

"Oh!" said Sher unbelievingly. Though he was not striving for anything from his service, least a chair like the one he was stuck to in the army for decades after the loss of his limb, the offer came as a pleasant surprise. He would love to continue the good work, albeit passively, he contemplated.

"That's the bad news. Wouldn't you like to know the good one," Mr. Verma was gazing at Sher intently. He seemed to be enjoying the little act.

"Oh! Sure," said Sher unsurely.

"You have been chosen for the prestigious "Extraordinary Achievement Award", an annual recognition, from among thousands of volunteers from all over India. It is for the conscientious and resolute effort to spread the vision of our organization and the comprehensive potable water usage data that you have collected by covering almost all areas in Delhi in the past four years. Considering ...your...handicap...it's indisputably extraordinary and astounding," beamed Mr. Verma.

"Thank you Sir, it's an honour, though I sincerely don't consider myself that proficient," said Sher Singh with humility.

"Sher, Let me tell you something, and I mean it: you are one of the most determined people I have known, and this recognition underscores that." Mr. Verma lit another cigarette. "The President of India will present the awards at a glittering ceremony at Siri Fort Auditorium next Wednesday, and your name is already on his list," he said.

"Is it possible for someone from our office to accept the award on my behalf?" asked Sher cautiously.

"Why?" Mr. Verma frowned.

"Nothing. It's just that I am not comfortable on stage or in front of a crowd," said Sher dubiously.

"Come on Mr. Sher Singh, you are a tiger and this is your award. Be there on time," Mr. Verma was disinterested in any further discussion on the matter.

"Come on Papaji, we will get late," Simran called out. She was overtly ebullient and excited about the felicitation. Every soul known to her had been informed about her father-in-law's big achievement and the date with the President. Sher felt irritated with her over-enthusiasm but then he patiently played along. They were, after all, his only family.

Deep was busy flipping the TV channels.

Honey sat on the couch, ostensibly bored. His father was unwilling to share the remote or switch on the cartoon channel. He loved his grandfather but dressing up for an award function where he would have to put on an armour of stiffness and decorum was not his idea of fun.

Sher Singh appeared in a navy blue suit that had been dry-cleaned for the evening. The suit had been stashed inside his heavy iron trunk for decades. The matching light blue turban and tie, chosen by Simran, augmented his personality. He felt awkward.

"Let's go," he nodded to his grandson, offering his index finger.

The seats were reserved for Mr. Sher Singh and his family. Attendants, scattered across the hall, were cordially directing the guests to their seats.

"Are you ok, Papaji?" asked Simran. Her father in law appeared drained.

"What?" he turned to Simran. "Yes…yes," he replied uneasily.

"Mr. Sher Singh," boomed the loudspeaker.

He got up slowly and walked to the dais, the walking stick knocked the wood on every step. Couple of attendants extended their arms on noticing the prominent limp, but Sher proudly waved to them to step back.

The President vigorously shook his hand and presented a neat certificate and a miniature metal shield. Sher bowed to offer his respect.

"May I?" Sher turned to the row of eager officials at a distance.

One of them hurried with a mike.

"I have something profound to share," the quiver in his voice instantly silenced the muffled disturbance emanating from diverse pockets in the audience. On one hand Sher Singh held the ornate metal shield with his name prominently embossed on it and firmly gripped the mike with the other.

He paused, as if in deep meditation. Only the whirr of the big oval fans could be heard.

"Thank you everyone for the great honour. I don't have words to express my gratitude, but let me be very clear about one thing. I don't deserve this trophy," Sher paused to catch a breath. The audience was stunned into silence.

"I have always dreaded the moment I would reveal my heart out", he began. "For decades, the dark secret was buried deep within my heart, but today I have to get it off my chest. The truth is that I resent myself."

"I have always urged people to conserve water," Sher continued, his voice shaking. "But no amount of water saved can wash away the stain of my past. I am a murderer. I left my friend to fend for him on that summer afternoon. I left him to die."

The room fell silent, every eye fixed on the vulnerable old man as he spoke.

'No amount of water I manage to save can quench Fateh's throat, who will always be thirsty, who has been searching forever for my water bottle which I promised I would leave behind for him, but I betrayed my only friend, the friend who took the bullet for me." Sher was trembling

"I am sorry Fateh! I am sorry! Please forgive me," he sobbed uncontrollably as flood of tears flowed down his wrinkled cheeks.

He knew he would never have that dream again.

Companions

"Is this seat taken?" she asked softly. She looked drained.

Surya straightened with a jerk by pushing the leg extension of the recliner. He removed the morning newspaper from the adjacent chair inviting her to take it.

The lady slipped her leather handbag from her shoulder and gently sat down on the leather recliner sofa chair. She appeared to be in her fifties though she had turned sixty-two in the previous month; her flawless skin, straight posture, black hair interspersed with patchy grey strands and an oversized red *bindi*, a tiny circular forehead decoration, common with Indian woman, made her conspicuously elegant. She wore a loose off white sparsely embroidered cotton *Salwar Kurta* with Roman sandals. Only a few wrinkled lines on her forehead and eyes clamored to declare her true age. Her large green eyes, with its explicit beauty and arcane gaze possessed the affinity to enchant any onlooker intrepid enough to engage them.

"Attendant to room no. 2131; attendant to room no. 2131," blared the speaker directly above them.

The ICU attendants' waiting area at Apollo Hospitals in Delhi remained perennially crammed with relatives, and any empty reclining easy chair was taken swiftly. The two hundred odd sofas, arranged in four long rows, were marked commensurate with the ICU patient's bed number, an order that was not followed, and the attendants occupied whichever they could lay their hands on. Some, stationed for months, would mark it as their fixed place for the duration of their stay. A mild fracas would occasionally emerge between an upright new entrant wielding his seat number and an old, temporarily permanent holder, the former eventually relenting to the desultory practice of being provided with an alternative by the staff.

"Attendant to room no. 2131, please report to the desk," repeated the prim young lady in official hospital attire from behind her table at the far corner of the lobby. The desk, stacked with several phones, a microphone and stationary to register entry/exits to the restricted ICU served as a communication point, between the ICU and lobby.

"I wonder where Mr. Rana is. They are calling out for him," said Surya and stood to survey the lobby, hoping to spot Mr. Rana.

"I guess he must have gone out for a breather," he smiled at the lady to his left.

Rhea gave a fleeting glance and nodded.

Surya was touching seventy and while his belly protruded alarmingly to stretch his striped polo neck T-shirt, his arms and legs were visibly thinner. He was almost bald save for a few strands that mushroomed above his large ears. His bony face shone with aliveness and energy, a result of years of honesty, hard work and a balanced life.

"Can you guard my place for ten minutes? Nature's call," he turned to her, raising his little finger.

"No, I am dead serious," he continued upon noticing her dubious expression, "it's difficult to reclaim the place once appropriated. Prized ones like these, which have greater leg maneuverability and are closer to the TV, have to be passionately guarded against ubiquitous opportunists who are raring to pounce at the first chance."

"Don't worry. I will," Rhea leaned back.

"Who is admitted...Your?" Surya treaded cautiously.

"My husband," she turned to him without hesitation.

"What happened?" he adjusted his frame to face her.

Rhea hesitated. Her quiet mundane routine has been suddenly transformed into frenzy and she was still in the process of calming her hysterical nerves.

"It's alright if you don't want to speak," Surya reached for the newspaper.

"No...No... Its fine, I guess. Early this morning, his infrequent breathlessness, which has troubled him throughout the latter part of his life, suddenly worsened and almost stifled him. It was terrible. "Fortunately, my daughter had come to our place after dropping her child off at school, and we could promptly rush him here," said Rhea gravely, her eyes fixed at a point as if the images of the morning were reenacting before her.

"You said he has had a breathing issue for a long time. Why?" Surya inquired, as if he were a doctor with all the time in the world.

"He has been allergic to dust, and the affliction intensified through smoking," she replied.

"So, he was a heavy smoker?" said Surya.

"In his heydays – yes, though through constant criticism and protest, mainly by his daughters, it had come down substantially. He always found ways to secretly abet his addiction," said Rhea with a hint of remorse.

"It's a repulsive habit; the most difficult to quit. Once a smoker, always a smoker, they say. How many daughters do you have?" Surya asked pleasantly to change the topic.

He was glad that the elegant lady was forthcoming unlike some stuck ups who are stubbornly unenthusiastic to converse. He could not complain as every single soul present was dealing with sadness.

"Three," she beamed.

"Working?" he smiled.

"All are married, settled and immersed in their busy lives. Two are working, dedicated to their career, while the youngest, the one who dropped me here, prefers to be a homemaker, directing all her energy on her adorable daughter. They are fine," she concluded seriously.

A sudden bustle ensued as some people scrambled together towards the flight of stairs at one end of the lobby that led to a door.

"Tea or Coffee?" asked Surya, getting up.

"For me? No…no…don't bother," she said unassumingly.

"What bother?? I am not going across the street. It's the afternoon tea from the hospital to us miserable creatures and though I must add that it's hopelessly bland but anything warm to soothe my throat and offer an activity is always welcome. And while I get the excitement, you have the other duty," declared Surya.

"To guard the seats," said Rhea.

"You already belong here," grinned Surya and walked towards the flow.

"How is the coffee?" he asked after Rhea had taken the first sip.

"It's fine," she smiled.

"Such an ambiguous word - "fine", reveals nothing to suggest that you liked it, could be taken as sarcasm or it could even signal disapproval or disgust with proper tone," chuckled Surya.

Rhea smiled broadly, "No…no…it's good."

The warm coffee soothed her. It was the first time she had smiled since morning.

Two beautiful ladies, one in her late twenties and the other approaching forty, hugged Rhea. Bereavement poured out of their melancholic expressions.

"You can sit here," invited Surya, getting up.

"No…no…it's fine…they can sit here…we can accommodate in one. The armrest is quite broad," objected Rhea.

"Don't be silly and formal. How can three ladies squeeze in a single sofa, pray tell me?" he enquired gently and mockingly. "Moreover I have to run across to the ICU and say hi to my wife; and don't lose the place," he warned before striding away.

From five to six o'clock in the evening, relatives could visit their patient one at a time. The resident doctor or nurse would generally provide a detailed update on the progress of one's patient. It was time to bring a smile to the patient's face in the midst of a maze of devices, tubes, incisions, and pain—or simply be by their side to reassure, connect, or develop strength.

"How is dad doing?" asked the younger daughter.

"Dinner?" Surya raised an eyebrow. He looked up at the wall clock in front, which said nine.

"I don't feel like eating," said Rhea without turning to him. Her daughters left around eight thirty after taking a peek at their father and urging their mother to be strong, to have faith and that the mild bump would soon be left behind. The younger one had brought dinner in a casserole to keep it warm and fresh, which lay in front of her in a jute bag, untouched.

"It's a ritual that is inescapable; food I mean. There is no other way," he smiled.

"What about you? We have been talking since morning and I don't even know your name. I am Rhea," she turned to him.

"Surya," he acknowledged.

"Richa, the younger one brought something," she said while picking up the jute bag. "Where is your ritual?" she teased gently.

"Oh! Don't worry about me. I will go out for a grab later. Some days I skip dinner to burn some of these," he grinned pointing to the sizable round girth. "Inactivity for so long coupled with junk food can only accelerate obesity. It's unavoidable I guess."

"I guess your wife is admitted. What happened to her?" she asked earnestly, putting the jute bag beside her legs.

"It was sudden. On her way down from the terrace, she slipped on the stairs in our house and lost control. Before she touched the bottom, her head banged against one of the stairs during the free fall. The internal brain hemorrhage resulted in total motor paralysis on the right side. No movement. Dead," he recited promptly as if it were by heart.

"Oh! I am sorry…it…" sympathized Rhea.

"No…no…. Why should you be sorry? You didn't have anything to do with it," he intervened.

"I mean…."

"I know what you mean," he assured her, "in fact, Doctors were genuinely surprised when she showed signs of quick recovery and this, they claimed, was noteworthy and rare, but then as luck would have it, she suddenly got infected by some potential drug resistant bacteria. Patients on a prolonged stay in any ICU are always at a risk of infection. Innumerable incisions drastically raise the risk."

"Oh!" said Rhea. She resisted the desire to sympathize.

"Her lungs got infected," continued Surya in a monotone, "which necessitates ventilator support – breathing assistance or else oxygen saturation to the brain drops alarmingly which can be detrimental. In layman terms, her lungs are not functional enough to deliver the minimum oxygen requirement to the brain. She is on life support."

"You certainly are informed," complimented Rhea.

"It's not a big deal. Today is your first day. You will get a thorough update from your doctor regarding your husband's progress and condition at least once daily. The more medical jargon a relative spits, the more time he has spent in these corridors. I hope you leave before you start mouthing these terms," said Surya dejectedly.

"How long have you been here?" asked Rhea.

"Six months," said Surya quickly.

"What? Six months!" exclaimed Rhea softly, "that's a long time to be in a hospital. But still your misery stands nowhere compared to your wife's. I mean your wife must be feeling terrible."

"She certainly is," he said softly as he felt a sudden moistness in his eyes.

"A few patients have clocked more than a year. For them it's just a long wait, I guess," he leaned back.

"Six months! My God, I still cannot believe it," she said, shaking her head.

"Does one really have a choice? The doctors occasionally raise your hope. What to do? Some days she is conscious, slightly alert while most of the days she remains too weak to respond. It has become a herculean effort for her to smile, both mentally and physically," he shook his head to conceal his glistened eyes.

The round metallic clock in front sounded a soft melodious dong. It was ten.

"See how time flies. That's how six months went by, without blinking," said Surya philosophically. "I think you should eat."

"Please assist in finishing it. I am sure Richa, extravagant as always, has stuffed much more than I can eat," she said as she reached for her jute bag.

"Lung Cancer, says the doctor; last stage. I wonder how it remained concealed for so long," she reflected grimly. Her wrinkled eyes were swollen and reddened due to unabated tears.

Surya gave a small nod, understanding that Rhea needed more than just hollow words of comfort or trite philosophical clichés. She needed someone to listen, to share the weight of her burden. It was only her second day in the new place, and Surya knew how difficult it could be to adjust to the unfamiliar surroundings.

After a restless first night, with incessant blaring of the paging system, it was clear that Rhea would need some time to acclimatize.

Surya had been absent for most of the day, and as a result, several of the other residents had approached Rhea, asking his whereabouts. They had noted the friendly conversation that the two had shared the day before and were concerned that something might be wrong.

Rhea had no answers for them, but as the day wore on, Surya eventually made an appearance, looking fresh and invigorated.

"What did the doctors say? I mean…how long?" he asked finally.

"They cannot confirm anything; 'everybody is different and responds differently' - were his exact words. From few days to a few months…" she trailed off.

"Can he go home?" asked Surya.

"Can he? I don't know. I never thought that was an option," she turned to him.

A tall, slim, middle-aged man came near and shook Surya's hand after bowing to Rhea. Surya immediately rose and shook his hands. He left a few minutes later after they ran out of common topics to expand on. Surya being a perky and an ebullient elderly was popular among attendants and several would call him every day to enquire about his wife or he would be flitting across the lobby to cheerfully engage in and share their sorrow.

"His father is inside for more than three months," said Surya pointing to the receding figure of the person he was chatting with. "The doctors have suggested that he can take his father if he so wishes. It has slipped out of their hands, they say, though I wonder if it ever was in their hands. Anyway he is uncertain about making the shift."

"What do you mean take him? Can he be shifted?" asked Rhea with concern.

"Not exactly, but then he might pass away more peacefully surrounded by his loved ones than with heaps of useless contraptions wrapped around his dying body," he said contemplating.

"But there is always a chance, a possibility. These doctors are not God who know everything and is it not illegal?" Rhea was clearly rattled by the idea.

"You are right. They are not God. It is we who aggrandize them. They are bound by the knowledge in the realm of the medical profession. They can only apply what they have learned which again would vary on individual competence and diligence. They have a limited scope of maneuverability," he said with clarity.

"I can agree on that, but why nonetheless give up on life?" she wondered emphatically.

"You have a point there, but then it's not that simple. Some families simply cannot afford it beyond a point and when, their God, the doctors themselves are hopeless, it really sets them thinking. You were saying something earlier about your husband?" said Surya, unwilling to be drawn into the sticky debate. He refrained from admitting that he fully endorsed her perspective.

"He is very sick," Rhea leaned back and closed her eyes. She was uninterested in any further discussion.

The bustle, the unending news of joy and sorrow and the propensity to doze off on the exceptionally soft easy chair, allowed time to slip through unnoticed.

A week had passed since Rhea joined Surya in the adjoining sofa. The staff inside the lobby, aware of their candid, amiable discussion and the brewing camaraderie, albeit transient, assisted to preserve their coveted seats.

"I have not seen anyone visiting your wife, apart from you…children?" wondered Rhea aloud after her daughters had left for the day. She had started to look forward to that part of the evening; the slot after the visiting hours and before dinner when the commotion would subside and their conversation was seldom disturbed.

"One cannot blame or demand from anyone. Everyone has to wash their own linen; there cannot be two ways about it. A single visit or a call exonerates friends and neighbors from the formality and as I said everyone is busy with their own agenda," claimed Surya.

He continued after a flicker of hesitation, "My only son is an American citizen."

Rhea sensed his aversion to elaborate when an uneasy silence ensued contrary to Surya's inclination to talk or have a perspective on any matter.

"I am sure you are in touch with him," prodded Rhea.

"He calls regularly to know about his mother's condition. He is doing well I imagine, busy as a result. He is sending money for the hospital bills, there is nothing to complain really," Surya justified uncertainly.

"What did the doctors say today?" she asked, diverting the conversation, much to his relief.

"Oh! It's hardly of relevance now. It has become a routine, a formality," he said plainly. "You can foretell with uncanny accuracy which of the few standard responses is going to come out, the moment he shapes his lips to speak. It's either - the condition is stable or the infection count is slightly higher and we have changed the antibiotics or the best one -she looks good today - don't you think? After six months of being in the thick of action, one knows that the doctors too have turned to the almighty for support and when the reins are in His hands, one can just relax," he smiled.

"But I see you very eager for the morning meeting," she reminded him.

"It is a high point of the day. Hope for a drastic deviation from the everyday monotone spurs me. That is all we have control over – prayer and hope," he looked down.

"One is always hopeful," she said.

"Yes, as the Old Russian adage goes – 'Hope is the last to die'," he agreed calmly.

"I overheard your daughter urging you to take a break today and have a good night sleep at home," said Surya while biting at his thick moustache at one end.

"They are concerned about my health," she said.

"In the last one month, I have not seen you taking a night off. You should listen to them," he asserted.

"I feel fine. Moreover I take an afternoon nap when I go for my bath, etc. The idea of the whole house to me at night still scares me. The swarm of people here, especially you, helps me to take my mind off the anxiety, the loneliness," she replied earnestly.

"I can understand," agreed Surya, "in the last six months, only once have I spent a sleepless night at home. I resolved to be here henceforth where my mind is and here I snore like a log," he laughed.

"And moreover I think it's inappropriate to request one of my daughters for an overnight stay. As you correctly pointed out the other day – all are embroiled in their own activities," she said.

"Very true," nodded Surya

"Sometimes I feel this phase should continue forever. I know it's criminal and borders on abject selfishness, but then the mind plays strange tricks," she shook her head.

"Let's go out for dinner, for a change," said Surya impulsively with a glint in his eyes

"Now?!" exclaimed Rhea.

"This is dinner time," reminded Surya.

"Are you asking me out for a date?" squinted Rhea, feeling her long hair with her fingers.

"Date it is!" declared Surya

"What? It is grossly inappropriate to even step into the ambit of such thoughts in our present circumstances," she opposed vehemently.

Surya peered into Rhea's anxious green eyes and said, "Most people here would concede to your contention but if I may put it bluntly, you and I have absolutely no control over the recovery of our loved ones, our prayers may, which again is debatable, but definitely not us by a long shot," he paused to reflect.

"Our austerity in such circumstances or hesitation to embrace life or be alive comes from our deep seated desire to control, which alas, is not our forte. We fool ourselves into believing that if we practice penance or control our desires, He would heed to our prayers out of turn. Allow yourself to let go, to be alive, come what may," he added forcefully.

"It is not that simple; what will my daughters infer if it reaches their ear?" she persisted.

"Look, Rhea," he said, coming closer, "you are going for food, not to an adventure tour to the Alps in Europe for fifteen days, leaving your critically ill husband behind. We humans have this unique capability to live our lives in our head, debating if's and but's forever, than actually hitting the road. Life is now and every moment is precious, which will never be repeated, a moment which is offering you a chance to be different. And deep inside, every human yearns to be different but rarely musters the courage," Surya was unstoppable.

He straightened and stood opposite her across the passageway with one elbow resting on the wooden platform where the attendants kept their belongings for the long haul.

After what seemed like eternity Rhea rose, straightened her *dupatta* to put it neatly across her neck and frowned, "Who will guard our seats in the meantime?"

The lobby was a place of sadness, the air thick with despair. Groups of residents could be seen huddled together, some openly expressing their grief while others remained stoic, as if their minds were shut down to any external stimulus.

Everyone in the lobby was consumed by a sense of loss and yearned for a way to escape the gloomy atmosphere. It was ironic that they longed for their previous monotonous lives, the very ones they had once cursed.

After dinner, Surya would usually sit in the lobby and watch the news on the large screen mounted on the front wall. The lights would be dimmed, except the one above the communication desk. Most of the attendants would be fast asleep.

Rhea reclined in the oversized armchair, her eyes closed as she tried to find some peace amidst the somber surroundings. It had been two months since that morning when she had rushed to the hospital, and time seemed to slip by in a blur.

"Do you still love him?" he asked after some time.

She opened her eyes and grimaced, "Excuse me?"

"Do you?" he asked without divulging any emotions.

She lifted her back and sat straight.

"What kind of question is that? Of course I do," she retorted, outraged as if it were irrefutable. The ambiance of serenity prevented her from uncharacteristically raising her voice.

Surya was unperturbed, "We have been talking for more than two months and the question had cropped in my head several times. I can sense a certain…how to say it…a certain impoliteness when you talk about your husband. I apologize if you think it is inappropriate and I have crossed the line."

He turned towards the TV screen.

"I stopped loving him a long time back," she started softly after some time, "so long back that I don't remember when was the last time I felt any passion or affection. I cannot claim to have lived a loveless life but then it vanished as if it were never there. There certainly was love when we began."

"Why do you say so?" Surya was absolutely attentive.

Rhea was relaxed as she searched inside for the response, "I am not sure, never really pondered; love takes a backseat in the turmoil for survival or pretensions."

Surya waited patiently.

She continued, "We were furiously passionate for a couple of years after marriage with eyes only for each other. It was euphoric as if we were a world unto ourselves and the world outside was irrelevant. The arrival of Dimple, our eldest daughter changed everything, which is understandable, but then the unshakable bond we shared developed irreparable cracks. Momentary sparks surfaced occasionally for some years but we could not hold on to it. I immersed myself in raising my kids and he, like a duteous husband, in providing for us."

"What you are recounting is not extraordinary. Priorities and responsibilities do creep in after the initial bliss of togetherness, and moreover raising three children is predominantly hectic than fun. I can understand.

Is that all?" he blinked.

"I guess so. We were an ordinary middle class family raising our kids, like everybody else around us. A life that is ordinary, normal," she exhaled deeply.

"Is that the reason for your.... malice... dislike?" Surya egged on.

"Malice..." she repeated inaudibly.

"I guess so," he was clinging to her every word.

"He never respected me," she whispered.

"Excuse me?"

"I hate him."

Surya did not interrupt the flow of thoughts, the catharsis that Rhea was experiencing.

Rhea wiped the thin sheen of tears from around her eyes with her *dupatta* before speaking; "He never missed an opportunity to ridicule me, to deride, to demean me in front of my children. He was ever prompt with proof of his smartness and superiority in any situation or argument. He always poured his frustrations on me for not reaching the top in his chosen career."

"Why would he want to prove that?" Surya frowned.

"He felt threatened by me. He knew I was professionally superior and he could never swallow it. I was a gold medalist in Economics from Delhi University with a promising career ahead.

Oh! I had so many dreams, so much to accomplish, all crushed for a life which amounted to nothing," she said dejectedly, blowing hard into her hanky.

"Do you hate him for making you feel inferior and being sarcastic at times?"

"No, for ruining my life," said Rhea with finality.

"How did he do that?"

"He never understood that I wanted to shine, to have my own mission," said Rhea irritatingly.

"Did you make it obvious to him that it was imperative for you to work?"

"No"

"Why not?" he wondered

"He knew when we were dating during college that I was keen to pursue a career," stressed Rhea.

"Maybe it was not that important for you?" he asked as if she were a witness on the stand.

"It was," she persisted.

"But you said you directed all your energy to raise your lovely daughters. Didn't you enjoy that role?" he asked.

"Certainly I loved being with my daughters when they were growing up. They would not budge an inch without me," she said with a sudden shine in her eyes.

"Maybe he saw immense potential in you, the great heights you could have scaled and when he saw you squander it to nurture his children, to make them your life, he might have felt that he had lost the women he loved," said Surya with compassion.

Rhea stared at him wide-eyed, dumbstruck, and unable to believe what she heard.

"It can't be that way," she was eager to discard the argument.

"And that could have spurred him to ridicule or criticize you so that you might be instigated to see your worth and be independent," continued Surya as if he had not heard the objection.

Rhea turned away from him and leaned back, staring straight ahead.

"Maybe he was struggling to provide for his big family, the leisure he dreamt of and wanted your supporting hand," he mused

"He did fine. Anyways I never complained," she replied quickly.

"Maybe you were content with the quality of your life. Maybe he wasn't," he spoke candidly.

Rhea shook her head. What Surya said did have a shadow of truth to it.

"Look here. I am not saying that it is the truth but it could be a possibility," he said kindly, "I am sure you had a fulfilled life bringing up your daughters to be mature, responsible and caring humans that I see they are. You have done a splendid job inculcating true principles in them and that should give you immense satisfaction. You could be regarded as a model mother, a mother always there for her children. You have lived each day doing what you really loved. You are among the few lucky fellows. There should be no reason to complain, but unfortunately there is."

"Why would you want to have a career or rather rant about having a career amidst all this bliss, when you loved what you were doing?" he asked again.

"I told you – I was proficient and could have really excelled," she raised her eyebrows.

"I am sure if you really loved Economics you would not have hesitated to take the plunge. What was the real reason?" he asked slowly.

"What is wrong with you? I told you," she alleged

"Why?" he demanded, like a lawyer towering over his defense witness.

"I wanted to show him that, if I worked, I would be far superior to him and that he was no match for me," she blurted loudly, violating the serene ambience and immediately put her fingers to her lips as if to prevent any further admission.

Silent tears streamed down Rhea's cheeks as she closed her eyes and prayed for forgiveness. She had always undermined her husband's tireless efforts to provide for their family. Although she never voiced her complaints openly, he could sense her dissatisfaction with the things he couldn't afford and instead of offering comfort, she would push him away. The gold medal in Economics would always be brought up in their heated arguments to silence him, but to her, it was just a piece of metal, and she could never muster the courage to embrace the life it represented.

What she really wanted was security, love, and provision, and he had never failed to provide any of those for her.

Suddenly, she longed to be by his side, to soothe his forehead, to plead for his forgiveness, and to love him again.

Despite her efforts to encourage her youngest daughter Richa to pursue a career and achieve financial independence, she always received polite rejection. Richa loved being a homemaker, much like her mother. To her, Rhea was the epitome of a fulfilled life.

It was time for her to accept the life she had lived and be at peace with it.

The guards stationed at the glass entrance fought hard to stall the blanket of sleep threatening to cover them in the early hours of the morning.

But for the couple in the first row, sleep was not a concern.

"Do you love her?" asked Rhea later. They were waiting for their coffee in the 24-hour coffee joint inside the hospital. Her face glowed like a newborn. It was two in the morning.

"What?" chuckled Surya, flashing his straight teeth.

"Do you?" she asked seriously.

"I have always loved my wife. If you were to be the model of motherhood, I would be that of husband-hood, if there were such a term," he said proudly.

"I have no doubts about that," smiled Rhea

"They say that love ebbs as marriage progresses but ours has only got stronger. We are inseparable, like one soul in two bodies. I don't know how I will survive without her," he signed for the first time in the evening.

"Do you really believe that she will recover fully?" she asked earnestly

"There is a chance. We can never be sure of His ways," he reasoned

"There is no doubt about that. But I am asking you what you think. I am sure you can see the terrible pain she is in; immobile for six months, needles being poked ceaselessly on the whims of our fancy specialists, for whom it's just another case. And you know better than me that it is no longer in their hands," Rhea said with a new found confidence.

"But…" muttered Surya

"You have to let her go," she said

"What?"

"Your attachment, your insecurity, fear of loneliness if she goes, is an obstacle for her to leave in peace. She loves you whole-heartedly and though enfeebled, is fighting to make it, to be with you but her body is not able to match her will. She knows she is fighting a losing battle, but then love knows no rationale. Nothing can be more heart breaking for her than to see you miserable, to know that she can no longer be with you, to know that it was she who broke the pact"

Rhea took Surya's hand in hers and held it firmly.

"True love is unconditional, unselfish like a mother's prayer, in defiance of the whole world, for the safety of her aberrant child," she said.

Surya placed his forehead on their joined hands and wept softly. "I want to remain selfish."

"It's time for you to bid her goodbye, for her to be in peace. She awaits your smiling consent, as she can never leave you sad. It's time for you to be free, so that she can be free."

Surya knew that it was time. He had known for a long time.

Rarely a lasting friendship or liaison gets molded in an ICU between attendants, the tenuous thread of sadness unable join them once they leave. Who would like to be reminded of those miserable days anyway?

That reality was about to be altered.

Cheesy Love

"RUN", shouted Zap to himself and dashed, stumbling and rolling, to a breach in a wooden cupboard in the kitchen. He could smell the unkempt toes nearby.

"Shhssshhh, don't move; that plastic is too loud; the 'big toe' is nearby," whispered Zap.

Zini struggled with the plastic, got entangled and finally was able to break free. She came and stood beside Zap. As she sniffed him, their whiskers greeted each other.

"What's wrong with you? You don't listen to me. I told you the big toe is around. He is awake and just outside," said Zap, exasperated.

"Oh! Don't worry; he is not bothered about us, he must be sneaking some sweets like us; hidden from the red toe," grinned Zini and chewed at the piece of plastic stuck between her two front teeth.

Zap peered at Zini and breathed a sigh of relief as he heard the retreating steps.

"Did you find anything to munch?" asked Zini turning away.

"No, the red toe is a maniac these days; she has become a cleanliness freak. It's becoming difficult to survive here. I don't know what has gotten into her. Every nook and cranny is spotless these days, as if the blessed Government has initiated some mandatory cleanliness drive. I could not..."

"I am so hungry!" signed Zini, disinterested in the explanation.

Zap did not respond. There was nothing to say; he was hungry too; but Zini was pregnant. He retreated to his corner and started licking his fore leg.

"I will have a look," said Zini and slipped out of the hole.

"What's for breakfast today?" asked Matthew with a toothbrush inside his mouth as he reached out and clumsily flipped the newspaper that lay on the low center table. Mathew was a heavy man with hefty round shoulders and a dense layer of coiled black hair all over his body. He carried a double chin by virtue of regular beer binges and his eyes were puffed out from last night's hangover. He was in boxer shorts and a white sleeveless vest.

"Don't talk to me while you are brushing. How many times do I have to tell you? It's disgusting," grimaced Angel.

"Hmmmm... I see," mocked Matthew and suppressed the urge to speak further.

"What's the matter with you these days; you just snap at everything I say?" asked Matthew. His brushing was complete and he sat beside Angel with his heavy arm across her thin shoulder.

Angel cringed but did not move away. Her full lips were pursed in annoyance. She was an attractive woman in her early thirties; high cheekbones and a curvaceous figure accentuated her charm further. Her hair was tied loosely in a bun with a wooden clip that was pierced diagonally. Two long tresses curled by the side of her brown eyes and touched her collarbone.

Their eyes—her expressionless and his eager—locked momentarily. Aroused by the closeness, Mathew suddenly pulled her and planted his lips on hers.

He was so immersed in his arousal that he failed to notice Angel's thin hands pushing him with all their might. She bit him hard on his tongue, which was trying to find an opening into her mouth.

"Aaargh!!" Matthew yelled as he recoiled, pressing the open wound with his finger.

"What is wrong with you these days?" he roared. "You have become too moody; don't tell me that your head is aching at seven in the morning. We seldom have time to do it at night due to our work schedule and you always seem….disinterested when we can. I have to…."

Angel was poking the decorated porcelain vase on the side table, indifferent to Matthew's tirade and that added fuel to the fire. What enraged him more was not the denial of his carnal desires, but the total disregard for his presence…his agony.

"What the fuck is the matter with you? Will you pay attention to what I am saying?" Mathew bellowed.

Angel looked up briefly, her eyes solemn, nonchalant and stared at him with an indifferent expression a moment too long and went back to her cleaning; picking at some hardened dirt on the vase with her index finger nail is what attracted her more.

Aware of the vase in Angel's hand and her capability to strike back, Matthew suppressed the urge to hit her

He kicked the sofa, inches from her long legs and stomped out.

"Anything?" asked Zap eagerly.

"Can you see anything?" snapped Zini. The pangs inside her stomach were slowly and steadily getting intense, though she could, with calculated risk, nibble on the biscuit crumbs that were scattered on the living room carpet, but it only aggravated her hunger.

"I see the red toe is cleaning like a maniac these days; what has gotten to her?" asked Zini to herself while scratching her head.

"I think we will have to take the risk." said Zap coming closer, his voice hardly audible as if someone might hear his grandiose plan.

Zini did not answer. She was losing her ability to think straight. The morning expedition and reconnaissance had yielded zilch.

"What is the matter with you, dear?" "We'll starve to death if we don't eat for another day; it's been more than a week since we've had anything substantial," Zap said softly, pulling at her whiskers.

"Which one?" asked Zini without looking at him. The lines of worry were clearly etched on her face.

"I don't know," said Zap. His pointed snout came closer, and he could feel Zini breathe. His eyes looked into hers, searching for a clue. He found none.

"Another shelter is fraught with menacing hazards. You know the dangers that crawl out there, big bullies, cats and the cold can become unbearable at night," said Zap trying to sound convincing

"And the other option is what…. a piece of cake?" wondered Zini cynically.

"No, a piece of cheese" said Zap, poking at Zini; "If we are careful, we might…" he desperately wanted to explain the brighter side. The very picture of a soft triangular piece of cheese between his teeth flooded his mouth.

Zini moved away gloomily, they have had these discussions innumerable times.

She will have to think for herself, she reflected.

"What??!!!" shrieked Anna wide-eyed, gripping the curved armrest for support. She had short hair, a prominent nose with thin lips and sunken cheeks. She sat on the edge of the wooden chair, her legs crossed and the denim short skirt she wore barely covered half of her thighs.

"When did this happen? What? Where? What is wrong with you? Have you gone crazy?" she blurted out, shaking her palms vigorously, maybe for more air as she could feel getting stifled with excitement.

"I have this strong urge to clean, to keep every corner spic and span since then. Dust is making me nausea tic," said Angel with conviction.

"What?!!! Does Mathew know?"

"Yeah, he knows I clean a lot these days. He can see that," winked Angel. "This morning he wanted to do it…you know…but all I could think of was dirt."

"Angel!!!" yelled Anna

Angel stared at Anna, mocking a serious expression and both of them burst into peals of laughter simultaneously.

"No, he doesn't," said Angel after regaining her prim composure.

"When are you going to break the scandalous news, darling?" Anna shifted to be more comfortable on the couch. She was enjoying the conversation, something to disseminate once she was out of the house, she thought.

"I will," said Angel looking down.

In an impulse Angel leapt from her couch, flung herself across, grabbed the wooden paperweight from the center table and propelled it with all her might. She ran out of the sitting room area, picked up her slippers on the way and threw it towards a pair of rats scurrying away from her. The rats, running for their lives, knew exactly where to head. They managed to escape the salvo of objects hurled at them.

Angel, looking behind her back, strolled back to the living room and slumped into the soft settee.

"What is wrong with you?" asked Anna, intrigued and bewildered.

"These two rats have been getting on my nerves for the past few days; the best cheese in town is hanging inside that rat cage; over there…can you see… for the past several days, but these smart assess have not even gone near to sniff it. I don't know how to get rid of them," signed Angel, contemplating the serious problem in hand.

"Get some pest control guy or company. There are so many available these days for a price," suggested Anna, peeved at the juicy gossip gone awry. "So, what were you saying about Mathews?" she asked indifferently, attempting to refocus on the sensational disclosure.

"I don't need any pest control company to get rid of a couple of rats. I have killed so many of them. I can get rid of them. I will have to think of something else," said Angel, picking up a cookie and not really listening to her friend.

"We were so close to the cookie lying on the carpet. I bet the red toe was unaware of it," said Zap, ruing the missed opportunity.

"But she was definitely aware of us. She almost got us," said Zini, licking her paws and sniffing the air around her.

"I guess we will have to move out of this place. We are not left with much option anyway. We might as well go out, look for food and perish rather than die a slow death here," said Zap, looking straight at Zini.

Zini did not respond. She was having difficulty concentrating with the hunger pangs growing in intensity every minute. She slumped into her corner and began nibbling at her long tail as her eyes closed involuntarily due to weakness and fatigue.

Zap went and sat beside her, their whiskers entangled, tails touching and nose sniffing the air for that elusive whiff of food.

"I am pregnant and it's not yours," said Angel casually. She was seated at her usual place in the sitting room.

Mathew, fresh after returning from his office had just picked up the TV remote.

"Excuse me?" he turned to face her, fully attentive.

"It's not yours. You heard me the first time," she said, observing the nails of her right hand from an arm's length.

Angel had anticipated a more shocking countenance, but Mathew's relaxed appearance disenchanted her and brought her back to the reality of their relationship. One corner of her mind was glad that Mathew was not animated and they might be able to settle this without tempers flaring or crockery flying across the room; Indifferently, if not amicably. What is wrong with Mathews, she wondered.

"Aren't you surprised? You seem to be…. fine with it," said Angel disbelievingly.

"Do you think I am a fool? That you would be fucking some smelly bloke from your office or the street and I would not smell a rat?" shouted Mathew, exasperated, not for the clandestine liaison under his nose but for being considered a dimwit.

"So you had known?" asked Angel calmly, ignoring the edge in his voice.

"I am sure the teenager in the next block knows more about your affair than me, though I had guessed something was amiss," mocked Mathew, settling in the chair in front of her.

"How?" squinted Angel, intrigued. She had tried to be immaculate in her stealthy affair.

"Never mind, if you care, I had noticed several other aberrations, like the muffled voice through the bathroom door when you would talk to your secret lover. The potty it seems is the most comfortable place to sit for those blissful conversations. "

"And you have been playing with it all along, unconcerned. Strange. That's definitely not how Mathew, I know, would have reacted. Considering your temper for trivial issues, I thought you would kill me if you had the faintest whiff. I am surprised…intrigued…to be honest. What am I missing here, Mr. Mathew?" mocked Angel, moving to the edge of the couch.

"Well," hesitated Mathew, "I have been seeing this girl in our office for the past six months and…."

"What!" "Which hairy whore have you been screwing behind my back, you bastard?" She jumped on the sofa. "Wait a minute. Now I get it," she exclaimed, pulling her hair back, "no wonder you've been conversing in monosyllables and nodding to whatever

I've said lately, but you know what? You will always remain a slimy, obnoxious bastard. You are..."

Wild guffaws halted Angel's barrage. Matthew, shaking his head, tapped his forehead several times with the remote that he was still clutching.

"What!" yelled Angel.

"Look...Look!" "Who's talking—look!" exclaimed Matthew between fits of laughter. He squeezed his eyes shut and clasped his chest to irritate her further.

"You are the one who drove me into this. You never cared for me or gave me time." "You are a selfish prick who only cares about himself," shouted Angel, raising her voice to pierce his laughter.

"What do you mean it's my fault?" I bet you had begun seeing this guy long before I started seeing Lindi. "In fact, my affair is only six months old, and I am sure that your new toy is older," squinted Matthew as he tossed the remote back on the centre table.

"Yeah, sure... but because of you. You are to blame for the state of our relationship," clarified Angel without any explanation.

"You are impossible." What did I do? You have all the comforts a woman could ask for here. I am not abusive. God only knows what you are saying, woman!" said Matthew, irritated.

"What about argumentative; you just want to thrust your viewpoint in all matters. You just don't listen; dominating; you are a typical male chauvinistic pig and off course insensitive.... to name a few," pointed Angel with a smug expression.

"Oh! So I am the bad guy here…hello, have you seen yourself in the mirror, Miss Perfect? You have driven me crazy all these years," Mathew snapped instantly.

"Bullshit! What did I do?"

"How about being stubborn for every small thing? You charge me with domination, huh? Who dominates most of the time, the type of food served in this house, the choice of music to be played, the amount of sex we should have. It's all as per your convenience and mood, lady. You would not have it otherwise. You prefer to nag your way in if something belies common sense or logic. And God! You drive me crazy with one of your sudden eccentric fussiness…like the cleanliness drive you have undertaken presently. I can go on expanding on your attributes forever," Mathew was unstoppable.

"I wonder how you are having an affair", said Angel under her breath.

"And what do you mean by that?" said Mathew raising an eyebrow

"Why do you think we are still childless after all these years?" asked Angel with a straight face

"What do you want Angel?" asked Mathew, calming down and not liking the direction of the argument.

"Now, Angel, we are both mature and responsible individuals. I know, somewhere down the line, we lost the fondness and affinity we once cherished. I think we are keen to do things our way. I know we no longer care for each other. I guess we didn't try hard, I don't know. I don't know what happened, but I reckon we lost interest in each other, got bored maybe," contemplated Mathew seriously.

"You are a bore Mathew", said Angel, relishing the upper hand. She seldom missed an opportunity to pounce.

"And you are a bore in bed," reacted Mathew instantly.

"Don't even go there, Mathew," glared Angel.

"Okay…Okay… we are not going anywhere with this belittling and the blame game. I guess we are alike in that we both want excitement elsewhere, though I see that you have been more serious about that", said Mathew. "Not that there's anything wrong with that", he added quickly.

"So, that's it I guess, we cannot survive together. We just lost it somewhere," said Angel, finally sitting back.

"Yes, we cannot survive together," agreed Mathew reaching for the remote, relieved that he could now switch on something more interesting on TV than his wife's annoying tone.

Zap's fingers caressed the cold aluminum metal grid; the spring-loaded lid was tightly secured. Little cheese was still hanging from the crude hook. Zini was pacing frantically, desperate for an opening to squeeze out. She had come and sniffed at Zap several times, though the greetings were ephemeral.

She must be too scared, Zap thought. But at least not hungry, he thought again.

He rued not being inside together with her, not for the cheese but to be together, to feel her with his long whiskers or scratch her back with his soft paws.

He would have to look for a new place. He might come across Zini again, who knows.

Zini had quietened, probably tired. She was staring at Zap. They were separated but the hunger had become utterly unbearable, she wanted to say.

Zap would understand, she knew.

Zap got up and looked at Zini; her eyes were fixed on him for the last time. It was dawn and the room was slowly getting brighter. He would have to move away.

They could not survive together.

Toys

"Madhu, the maid is here", said Mrs. Patel as she opened the front door.

"Hmm", nodded Madhu without looking up from the newspaper she was reading.

Sheila entered, bowed casually to no one in particular and turned towards the first floor to clean the apartment, as she did diurnally. She stopped abruptly in her tracks on hearing her name boom through the staircase. With trepidation, she slowly turned around.

"Who is this?" Mrs. Patel asked disapprovingly, towering over the small child. Her big arms were folded to elicit authority.

Sheila's miniature and frail frame struggled to look up. It was only her head that moved, but the effect was as if the whole body felt the pain, as if the body resisted the movement. Her forehead was lined with several permanent creases while her small tired face illustrated years of labour and struggle to eke out a living. Her somber eyes had sunk deep into their sockets while her cheekbones protruded pointedly above the dry cheeks. A thick layer of vermilion adorned her neatly parted hair. She wiped the small beads of sweat below her nostrils with her bright sari and stared at Mrs. Patel with fearful eyes.

"Who is this, Sheila?" frowned Mrs. Patel, unaware that the cynicism in her tone was preventing the answer. Sheila looked down and fidgeted while the child frowned in defiance.

Madhu, all ears for the unusual conversation, suddenly lost interest in the paper. She came and stood beside her mother-in-law, scanning the small girl beside Sheila.

"I…I…I…thought I would bring her along. It's Sunday and we can finish faster and she has no school today and she will not touch anything." Sheila gasped, staring at Madhu. She was unprepared for the enquiry.

The little girl in an oversized frock stared all around her with big intent eyes. She had a small face like her mother, full nose and dense hair that almost touched her thin waist. At first sight, with a deep discerning gaze and calm composure, she came across as precocious.

"She is your daughter?!" she asked knowingly.

Sheila nodded. She wiped her face again with the edge of her sari.

"But don't make it a habit…Ok", warned Mrs. Patel. One of her principles advocated being strict with household helps.

The duo disappeared into the stairs.

"One has to be careful of them; that little girl, she must be what – eleven, twelve… she can pick things and we would never know", said Mrs. Patel to Madhu and herself. "You must keep an eye on them."

"I don't like Sheila," scoffed Madhu "She is not sincere with her work and moreover, is always requesting for this or that. Yesterday she asked me for some vegetables. God! Can you imagine? The other day she requested clothes. Once in a while it is fine, but every day! That's irritating. Poonam was better," she claimed, referring to the previous help who had quit a week earlier.

Sheila went about her chores in a mechanically frantic pace; her way of working. If she chose to be diligent or painstaking, she would not be able to finish all the houses that she knocked in a day.

Radha stood near a stool in a corner observing several portraits in oil canvas that filled the wall opposite to her. All seemed to be staring at her, she thought.

"Don't stand there and suck your thumb", shouted Sheila from another corner of the house, without any notion as to where her daughter was, "come and help me".

Indifferently, Radha looked up to confirm the direction of the voice. She had cursed her mother when coerced to follow her. She would have preferred to loiter in her nighbourhood with her gang, playing marbles, chasing the chickens or picking guavas from the neighbour's tree.

Her eyes went to several small plastic animals strewn on the floor. The assorted wild animals were approximately two inches in size, moulded intricately to give a fine finish. The facial features were well defined. She picked one and made it stand on the wooden table with a glass top that lay in the center of the room.

The infant, hidden behind a curtain in one corner, had been observing Radha all along. She could not contain herself any longer. With a finger between her two front teeth, the child ambled to the table and stood near Radha. With one palm stretched on the table for support, she looked inquisitively to welcome Radha. Shall we play? She wanted to say to her amiable friend.

"Show her your toys darling", smiled her father, staring adoringly at her daughter. He sat in one corner of the sofa while his nimble fingers tirelessly punched the keys on his mobile.

"Yes?" "Yes?" she tweeted. It was one of the dozen words she had mastered within two years of her arrival to the blessed planet.

She ran to the middle of the room, collected the other wild animals scattered on the floor, some from seemingly inaccessible corners and dumped them in front of Radha.

"What is that?" sang Suresh, "cheetah", came the prompt reply.

"And that", "Elephant"."

"And this", "Hippo." "NO!"

"Giraffe?" "NO!"

"Rhino?" "Yes," beamed the proud father.

He pulled her for a hug but the child resisted. She wanted to play with Radha.

Radha stood there expressionless, staring at the toys, mesmerized. Though she was eleven years old and went to the local government school, she could only recognize the elephant.

She was in love with the toys.

On the way back to their house, Sheila walked faster while Radha struggled to keep pace. It was two in the afternoon and Sheila's day was still lined with several unfinished chores before she would be able to have lunch.

Her elder brothers were not at home and father, who seemed flushed, was snoring menacingly when they opened the door.

"How much would those toys cost?" asked Radha after they had eaten their lunch; rice and some *dhal* floating on water.

"What toys?" Sheila squinted.

Radha stared at the ground, continuously making imaginary circles with her fingers. "The one in the house with the baby," she replied without looking up. She knew her mother was about to lose her patience.

"What toys? And is this your age to play with toys? When will you start helping me with work? I think you should stop going to school and come with me; what is the point of school anyway? It's just a farce. We are destined for hard labour and poverty," she bellowed furiously.

Sheila left Radha with her circles. She was in no mood for a discussion.

"How many times have I told you to be a little early?" asked Mrs. Patel with a straight face and pursed lips. "Is this the time to come?" *If she hits me hard, I might need an ambulance,* thought Sheila.

"Mrs. Singh had too many utensils from last night's party, madam. I got delayed there," said Sheila in her characteristic loud tone that came naturally when she thought she had a valid alibi.

"I will not tolerate this for long," snapped Mrs. Patel, persisting with her tirade.

Sheila nodded. The risers on the stairs seemed higher than the day before, thought Sheila. *'It's taking me ages to climb today,'* she contemplated nervously.

"Now how do I find those animals in this maze," thought Sheila, scanning the room full of toys in different hues and shapes that were scattered all around.

"Can I have a glass of water, *memsahib*?" asked Sheila picking up her cloth bag.

"You are always asking for something or the other. Here, take. Poonam never asked for anything," said Madhu, getting irritated.

"How come Memsahib gave you these toys?" asked an excited and animated Radha as she gaped at the small plastic animals.

Her mother smiled and muttered some gibberish under her breath. Anyway Radha was not listening. She had become one with the toys, examining them in detail. She laid them out on the floor and began to talk to them. She made the horse gallop over the rickety wooden stool; made the cheetah stare at the giraffe and the lion devour the deer with a high-pitched roar. "Ravi must be familiar with all of them. He goes to that expensive school in the next colony. I will ask him the names in the evening," she smiled feverishly.

It was her first bunch of toys in thirteen years of her existence. She would sleep with them tonight and every night.

"Have you seen baby's animals? I can only find three of them," asked Madhu while applying *Mehendi* on her scalp in front of a small portable mirror kept on the centre table in front of her. The herb was supposed to thicken and improve the texture of her hair.

"I don't know. It must be around somewhere. Have you looked under the sofa?" replied Suresh without looking up from his computer.

"I have looked everywhere," snapped Madhu on being asked the obvious question. "Baby likes to play with her animals, it's one her favorite pastimes," she said, adjusting her face in front of the portable mirror.

"It must be somewhere here," repeated Suresh without sounding convincing or interested.

"I think Sheila has taken them. Her daughter was quite interested in them the other day. I don't like Sheila at all; she is not good at her work and is always imploring for things. She makes such a sorry face but is manipulative to the core, that is the only ace up her sleeve, to play the victim," Madhu could not resist the opportunity to portray the picture playing in her mind.

"Why would she steal the toys?" Suresh was suddenly alert.

"I know she did," came the curt reply

"That does not explain much. I saw her daughter that day.... but why was I in the house...aha...it was Sunday," Suresh tapped the back of head as if to spur his brain into activity. "She is quite old for those toys...I don't think so...you are overreacting," he said resolutely.

Madhu's revulsion for the timid maid was growing steadily with each passing day, while on the other hand Sheila went about her chores, unaware of the scrutinizing gaze. She wanted her replaced at the earliest. She was confident that Sheila had stolen the animals.

"Mama, where is the Giraffe?" the baby asked, stretching each word.

"Come, give mama a hug," said Madhu.

"I want the giraffe! Giraffe!" the child wailed.

She had searched everywhere in vain. She wanted to kill Sheila.

Radha had become inseparable from her fine quality toys. Her eyes glowed when she woke up to them lying beside her every morning, neatly arranged in a row. She would kiss them individually like a mother gently waking her child for school with a peck. She would proudly flaunt her 'animal friends' to her neighbourhood gang and take pleasure in their envy.

"Why do you have to come early from school? Those animals are not going to run away," Sheila confronted Radha, who was busy feeding grass to the giraffe. Sheila did not prod further as she knew sooner or later Radha would have to join her to make ends meet and later, after marriage, slog for her own family. Typically, girls in their community tied the knot upon touching the legal age or maybe before. A few more years and both of them would be on their own, signed Sheila.

Sheila had begun to sense the contemptuous eyes following her around the house as she brandished the broom with practiced ease and wiped the floors. She knew Madam did not like her but then nobody did. A quivering voice within her told her that Madam suspected her of theft.

"While cleaning, have you seen the animal toys that the baby used to play with?" enquired Madhu nonchalantly, unable to resist anymore.

"No Madam," she said, avoiding a direct stare.

"Are you sure? Because, suddenly they are missing and you are the only outsider who is familiar with every corner in this house," said Madhu, raising an eyebrow.

"Yes Madam," said Sheila, praying for the ground to split and engulf her or Madam to get distracted.

"Those animals had remained scattered all over the place for the past six months and after a month of your arrival, I find them missing," insinuated Madhu in a restive tone.

It had been three weeks since that fateful day. Sheila knew that one day she would have to face the inevitable question and had rehearsed the reply several times in her head.

But she could not find her voice and stared at Madhu.

Madhu did not repeat the question. She stared hard as she waited for Sheila to respond.

Sheila snapped back from her trance and gathered her wits, but her response turned belligerent instead of the calculated answer that she had practiced.

"What are you saying Madam?!!! How can you say that?!!! We may be poor but are not thieves and our kids don't have time to play with toys," she could hardly control her breadth.

After what seemed an eternal silence, Madhu turned her back. She knew that the toys were gone forever.

The walk back home appeared unusually longer that evening. Sheila knew she blew it and it was only a matter of time before she would be shown the door at Patel's residence. She did the same work at four households and cleaned the utensils at Mrs. Singh's. The loss of Patel's household would mean a deduction of thousand rupees from her monthly income. That would pinch her. Though her husband worked as a guard in a bungalow in one of the plush areas that she could not pronounce, he would fritter away his earnings in local spirits and an occasional visit to the brothel where he was considered a regular, eligible for some discount. On occasions he would force his reeking self on her to turn limp a few minutes later. Sheila never resisted, either to avoid a ruckus or getting thrashed. Her two sons had declared their aversion to school the moment they hit their teens and avidly earned their pocket money from cleaning cars every morning in the locality where she worked. Infrequently they would get fortunate and clean a drain or dirty tank in one of the houses, earning enough to enjoy a good meal at the local Dhaba in the evening.

But why was she concerning herself with all this, Sheila wondered.

All her internal conflicts evaporated the moment she spotted Radha, playing with her animals, outside the small door of their one room cubicle. She was her favorite. Sheila saw her childhood in her, fearless and carefree. All the animals were christened. The elephant, Jumbo, with dark maroon back, off white legs and trunk raised to the posture of an elephant's call, was her favourite.

That evening while removing a bowl of boiling water from the clay oven, she stepped on Jumbo, stumbled and spilled the container over her right forearm. Radha rushed her mother to a local physician who bandaged the burnt region with care and instructed her against using her right hand for a week. Sheila's vehement protest only elicited a cold stare from the aged Physician.

A week later, Mrs. Patel politely asked Sheila to stop coming as they had fixed another maid. Sheila argued her case and demanded to know the shortcomings in her work but Mrs. Patel was not in a mood to relent. She had been absent for a week without intimation when only a couple of days of leave were allowed in a month. She showed her charred arm and begged for reconsideration but Mrs. Patel had made up her mind to utilize the golden opportunity to get rid of the unclean maid.

A few years later Radha was married to a young carpenter, who lived in the same colony and belonged to their caste. She had packed the toys well in advance.

"Keep those animals on the shelf. Now!" yelled Radha at the top of her lungs.

Raja, her six-year-old son, however, ran away from her mother and jumped into the lap of his frail grandmother who yelped at the sudden impact. His mother was never concerned about his other toys, but those animals evoked a fit in her. Raja had chewed off one of elephant's legs when he was an infant; the giraffe's tail was missing, but his mother's eyes still gleaned whenever she sat with them and that really fascinated him.

Sheila, who had become old and coughed badly throughout the day, smiled at her grandchild indulgently. She stayed with her younger son, who worked as a chauffeur. She was on one of her weekly visits to Radha, which was normally on a weekday to avoid her son-in-law.

"You still have those animals," she whispered to herself, staring at the scar on her right forearm. *They didn't heal completely*, she thought, running her fingers over them.

"Yes Ma," said Radha, looking at her mother in the eye. "They are my only real friends. They are my world and I cannot live without them."

Sheila hesitated. She had always wanted to make a clean breast of it but could not muster enough courage. She may not live long and the thorn, which had been pricking her for years, had to be removed from her fragile chest, she mused.

"I…I" she started, "stole those toys that day," and finished after a few moments.

Radha came and sat beside her mother who was looking away. She gently turned her mother's face towards her with her palm and smiled. Sheila's eyes were moist and Radha could sense the deluge of tears waiting to break through. She had not seen her mother weep, no matter how grave a misery she faced. She was much like her mother, she thought, tough, indomitable.

She rose slightly and embraced her mother for the first time in her life and after sometime spoke, "I know Ma, and I have always known and loved you more for that."

Sheila wept uncontrollably and felt like a feather.

♡

Unrequited Love

He placed his right palm on her soft thighs and it remained there as he guffawed loudly, "Ha… ha… ha…. ha… ha…I am sure he would double check his balls before attempting another delivery at your place…ha…ha…ha…or you can…you know…ha…. ha…. ha…squeeze them next time…. ha…ha…ha."

"Ha…ha…ha…ha," she followed.

He clutched his stomach, doubled over in laughter, and pushed away from the wooden headboard. Kimaya sat next to him on the bed, her feet touching the floor. Tina forced a small chuckle, though her eyes glared at her husband's hairy hand on Kimaya's tight cotton slacks. Her heart pounded like a woodpecker's beak against a tree, and her palms grew sweaty despite the adequate air conditioning. Sitting next to her husband, she folded her legs and busied herself with a pile of dry clothes.

"Oh! God!" he huffed. His arm pressed on Kimaya's thighs to form an irregular cavity as he leaned towards her to raise his other arm to gently massage his eyelids and squeeze the remaining water out from his eyes. Tina swallowed a lump as she felt her heart racing away.

Though Kimaya was in her late forties and a mother of two grown daughters, her immaculate skin and short hair styled like a schoolgirl's, hid her age by many years. Although she became hefty and could not regain her distinct curves after the birth of her second daughter, Kimaya was an attractive woman with full breasts, thin shapely nose and beautiful eyes. A prominent mole on her chin, amusingly referred to as 'a beauty spot' by her, instantly magnetized any onlooker's gaze to it.

"I will be on my way," said Kimaya, turning to Tina.

"Yes? Ok! … Home?" Tina regained her demeanour before either of the two overtly friendly pair could get a whiff of her disquiet. Tina kept her fluffy dense black hair at shoulder length. Her thick eyebrows, broad nose and thin upper lips curved slightly to the left when she smiled, giving her a sensuous appeal. She hated her huge thighs that were a cause of embarrassment for her in tight pants or tracks.

"Hang on for some more time. It's only…what…twelve," requested Ray as he switched the position of his palm to his own thighs. Ray was concerned about his receding hairline and was always on the hunt for new hair growth remedies or any new breakthrough technology. He desperately desired to shed a few extra pounds around his waist as well but the conviction would wane after a month's rigour and forced discipline. Tina, after years of nagging, had given up.

"I would love to but have to go and cook. Deb is coming for Lunch today," she smiled as she rearranged her stole.

"Ok…I will see you to the door," said Ray, jumping out of his bed in one swift motion.

"Relax. I am just going next door," said Kimaya, pushing him back.

"It's Ok," he insisted.

"Bye Tina," she waved smilingly.

"Bye," she feigned a smile.

The simple, undemanding ritual of arranging clothes appeared to be excruciatingly difficult. Tina flung them aside as her mind, caught up in an emotional frenzy, pushed her in a variety of ways. Looking straight ahead, she took a deep breath to calm her agitated mind before it could begin to spew its venom, which had a proclivity to get ugly and out of control. One corner of her head was grateful that Ray had been obstinate to follow Kimaya. If Kimaya had left alone, leaving them together, she would have inevitably exploded.

Tina had no reason to believe any promiscuity or immoral intent between the childhood friends; in fact, over the years, she had grown to admire Kimaya's courage and boldness to take charge of her life on her own terms after her husband's untimely demise. Single handedly she had struggled to effectively balance her work and raise her daughters to be principled, confident and above all, brazen to take on life.

Over time an intimate and reliable friendship developed between the three. Tina had felt initial pangs of jealousy in the early days of her marriage, intensified mainly due the childhood history of friendship, but after knowing Kimaya more closely, she was left with only admiration for her.

But these sudden physical gestures and proximity, like today unnerves her. They had been married for fifteen years. A sense of insecurity tiptoed to take firm root. *'Is Ray looking for some spice or is he just plain bored with me?'*

She wears such low necklines to reveal her ample cleavage. How can a man not get ideas at such close range? And the blitz of contradictory poignant thoughts continued.

"Happy Birthday to you…. Happy Birthday to you…" the ensemble sang and clapped without taking their eyes off the creamy chocolate cake. A thin undulating streak of smoke was still rising from a few extinguished candles.

As the *birthday song* subsided, Deb sliced a small piece of cake, offered first to her mother, followed by Nikki, her younger sister and devoured the remnants.

Ray, as feisty and joyful as ever at any social event, took the slim plastic knife, sliced off a fair portion, and shoved the chunk on Kimaya's face, vigorously smearing the cream on every inch of her face; before the unsuspecting gathering could react incredulously. Ray's left hand immediately extended to assist her as she stumbled from the abrupt contact. "Ray!" she exclaimed. The guests applauded as Kimaya yielded to the quirkiness after a meek and tentative protest.

Suddenly, her leather slipper stepped on a piece of cream; she slipped and twisted her ankle. Ray's other hand glided across her bare abdomen as he leaned in a flash, to prevent an awkward and heavy fall. She desperately seized the cuffs of his shirt and pulled herself up. He gave a strong jerk to pull Kimaya up, squeezing the air between them as their chest pressed against each other. Kimaya stiffened. She could feel his hot breath on her ear that sent a tingling sensation down her neck. The gang surrounding the couple had turned silent as if in a trance, awaiting their next move. Someone clapped and the room exploded into a loud applause. Some of them giggled at each other. Kimaya gently wriggled out of the hug and picked up the loose end of her *Sari* that had fallen to the ground. She pushed it behind her back in a swift motion and apprehensively surveyed her friends.

"Mom, are you all right?" asked Deb gingerly, softly squeezing her shoulders.

"I am fine," Kimaya smiled nervously. In fact she felt great.

Some of her friends and colleagues came near her to confirm her safety, teasing her with a piece of cake in their hand.

Kimaya pointed at her face and said to no one in particular, "I will clean and be right back."

Deb nodded. She could vouch that her mother's beautiful eyes had turned watery. She thought it was peculiar for such a trivial mishap. And Uncle Ray had always been a prankster.

No one noticed another set of eyes in the room that was fighting to hold back fury.

"What was the need to splash cake on Kimaya's face?" glared Tina. She had been boiling ever since they had returned from the drab party. Everything seemed dull to her after the cake incident and she took a plate to appease Kimaya who kept a stern eye to ensure that all guests were lavishly served. Tina hardly ate anything. After the kids were cozily tucked inside their blankets, she knew she could not hold it further.

"It's just a small trick to liven up the party. We used to do it all the time in school and college," Ray said casually.

"Do you think everyone was amused, that everyone there enjoyed it?" Tina felt the faint tremors of an impending earthquake about to rock inside her.

"Oh! It was nothing. "I told you we used to surreptitiously splash cake from behind," he said, engrossed in his novel. He lazily lay in his favourite position, with his legs straight and his back supported by the bed.

"So why didn't anyone join you in the fun?" she asked sarcastically. His nonchalant answers were infuriating her.

"Some were eager to, but Kimaya tripped, and the moment was lost," he said after giving it some thought.

"Do you think Kimaya loved it?" she squinted from her side of the bed.

"She was alright with it," he said, turning a leaf.

"What do you expect her to do? Throw a tantrum and kick you out of the house in front of everybody," she retorted quickly.

Finally Tina's harsh tone caught up with him. He looked sideways at her to face a grim and serious expression.

"What is the matter? Why are you taking it so seriously? It was Kimaya's birthday and I applied some cake on her face.

What is the big deal? I will drown your face in cake on your birthday, if that is bothering you," he said earnestly.

"Do you find her attractive?" Tina blurted, not really listening to her husband.

"Always have," said Ray reactively and immediately regretted it. The course of Tina's enquiry was becoming evident but Ray chose to neglect it.

"Then why didn't you marry her? She was once your best friend and sometimes I get a feeling that she still is," she asserted cynically.

"Why are we having this discussion at this unholy hour? It's past twelve!" said Ray, putting the book aside.

"I don't believe that you did not have feelings for her," she charged, ignoring the unholy hour jibe. For her, it was the best time for the discussion.

"We were neighbours. We still are. We went to the same school, at times sitting together in the same class. It was inescapable to be friends, given the circumstances. And what is wrong with that?" Ray was fishing for a way to end the uneasy conversation but he found himself getting sucked deeper into it.

"Do you want to do it with her?" Tina dropped the bomb.

"What?" Ray pretended innocence. The specter of a prolonged argument and a restless night on the sofa loomed large.

Tina stared at him to let the question sink in.

"What has gotten into you? You dimwit. I have known Kimaya for almost forty years, maybe more. If something were playing in my mind, it would have taken shape eons earlier," he barked, sounding unconvincing.

"How do I know what's playing in your mind?" she shouted, refusing to be intimidated.

"We have a family. Our kids are growing beautifully. Why do you want to rake an inconsequential issue and make a mountain out of a molehill?" Ray toned down.

"You mean, to feel or press a woman's thighs is perfectly normal?" she pulled out another arrow from her quiver.

"What do you mean?" he was mildly surprised this time.

"Lately, I see that you touch Kimaya all the time…maybe you don't realize…I don't know…that too right under my nose…. in our bedroom!" Tina grimaced. She raised her arm in exasperation.

"It's nothing," he rejected the charge outright, suddenly remembering the exact instant being referred to.

"Would you be comfortable if an old friend of mine visits us and I throw myself on him, touching him all over? Would that be acceptable to you?" she frowned.

The idea of a reversal in roles appalled and unnerved Ray. Male Chauvinism is deeply ingrained in our culture; its roots can be traced back to the time when humans separated as a species from their four-legged kin. He invented his own tools and fought with animals in a tussle for food and land. As his success grew, he became possessed with the desire to be in control, to be the patriarch, and any voice of dissent from the fairer sex would be annihilated mercilessly. Women, who were noticeably softer and tenderer in an era when physical might ruled, were involuntarily relegated to humble chores such as caring for the house, children, and so on—chores that continue to this day with a euphemistic label. They resigned or tacitly agreed to the role of a subordinate to feel more secure in the harsh outside world teeming with other chauvinists, and they still do. An unsaid bargain was reached. And in his tough avatar, he declared himself superior, and that pledge still echoes in our genes.

Ray's silence said it all. He gazed at Tina with irritation for hiding an ace up her sleeves. She waited impatiently. His controlling self would not give that freedom to Tina, no way, he thought. It was his responsibility to call the shots after all.

He rose swiftly without warning, wrapped a couple of pillows and a thin sheet in an untidy bunch and walked out of the bedroom without a word.

The sofa in the living room always came to his rescue.

As friends sharing a common boundary wall, Ray and Kimaya were inseparable during their childhood. Every morning they walked to the same Primary School in Rajendra Nagar, a spread out colony in Patna, the capital of Bihar, a small state in Eastern India. They sat together in class. After School they would be at either place, spending the hours playing carom, chess or indulging in the pile of comic books stacked in Ray's room or tirelessly trying to solve that day's quick crossword. Ray ignored the blatant insinuation from his peers of being effeminate whenever he was spotted with Kimaya. Since the age of twelve, he was in love with her unabashed free spirit.

"Are we meeting in the evening today?" asked Ray, as they walked towards their home after school.

"I don't know," Kimaya turned to him. Her long hair was neatly plaited. "Board exams are a few months away. Mom keeps reminding me whenever she crosses me. 'Study! Good grades are a necessity' she shrieks. Even Dad joins her during dinner," she complained.

"Good grades in twelfth is essential if you want to pursue normal graduation, else if one is confident about cracking one of the competitive exams, plain passing marks should suffice," said Ray seriously as if he had a clear vision for his future.

"But it's still called board exams," said Ray. "And who would explain that to my fuddy-duddy parents," she said

"I know," he nodded.

"Ok. See you," said Kimaya, as she opened the main metal door to her porch.

"Yeah. See you," smiled Ray.

"How come?" asked Ray, as Kimaya entered his room later that evening.

"My parents had to go for a get together," grinned Kimaya, as she slumped on his ornate bean bag near his study table.

"But that's not fair. They must be imagining you surrounded with books," said Ray.

"I just came by to say hello. I will go if you so desire," said Kimaya, making herself more comfortable.

"But…" he said weakly.

"No buts. Come and sit here," said Kimaya, pointing to the empty chair.

Ray was still standing. Fearless Kimaya; like a spell, he was magnetized to her boldness and followed her like a slave. Rumours branding them as a couple had grown louder in school. A puritanical liaison was inconceivable by his classmates, the girls being more vociferous in poking. Occasionally, complacency overtook him when his mates openly lauded him for having a girl.

Slowly, he made his way to the chair near her. As he turned to her, fresh fragrance from her still wet hair permeated his being. She sat cross-legged; her mini skirt exposed her thighs more than it covered while the thin-strapped sleeveless t-shirt ran parallel to her transparent pink bra-straps. Of late an internal conflict brewed whenever they found themselves together in his room and he struggled to quell the sensual impulses. To say that he frequently fantasized himself knotted in a passionate dance with her would be an understatement. His senses were enslaved to the wild images of ecstasy and his longing to drown in her curves was like a man's desperation for water in an interminable desert. He had pulled himself on several occasions earlier, fearful of the repercussions, scared of being admonished and shunned by Kimaya. What if Kimaya labeled him repulsive, despicable and loathed him? He loved her company more than anything else and was unwilling to fritter it away.

"You take a lot of stress Ray. We have known each other since the age of five, maybe earlier. And we are not up to any mischief; we know that. We cannot help it if our parents feed their mind with unrestrained fantasy about us," she giggled as their bare shoulders touched.

"Mischief…?" he breathed slowly. He knew he might not be able to control his visceral desires in an opportune setting for long.

Their eyes met and held the stare unblinkingly. Their eyes, in that moment, conversed explicitly, bringing forth their deepest desire like no words ever could have. Ray felt his heart beating wildly and a profound sensation gripped his abdomen. They could feel their heavy breathing on their sensitive cheeks. Her striking mole appeared blurred at such close proximity. His lips softly touched her glistening lips, while one hand slowly glided to grip her waist. He could sense her tense body gradually giving in as she moved forward and parted her lips to cover his. With eyes shut, their lips, tongues teased and played as they kept biting and kissing each other. 'Have you gone crazy?' boomed a voice inside him. It was crushed instantaneously. He was sure that Kimaya was experiencing a similar dilemma, but the catharsis of passion was unstoppable. He was over the moon that Kimaya harboured exact emotions.

He pushed back the chair as they stood up together, violently kissing each other, his right hand caressing her back while the left gently guided her to the edge of his bed. He removed his loose sleeveless T-shirt with a jerk and helped her pull out her soft cotton top. The tight, transparent bra pressed her firm breasts to form a deep crease in the middle. Ray adjusted a couple of pillows in a line. Their eyes met again to search for any guilt, hesitation, or fear. Kimaya giggled, removed the band to loosen her long hair, and jumped on the bed. Ray moved beside her on his single bed, kissing her neck and lips and squeezing her breasts as she moaned with her hands around his neck. He drew one leg, caressed her inner thighs, pressed them against his hands, and rubbed the soft skin. Her soft breasts wobbled out of the bra cups as Ray pulled them down. He squeezed and pressed her breasts, kissing and nibbling at each nipple in turn. "Softly..." breathed Kimaya, as his teeth dug into the soft nipple in his wild frenzy. Kimaya was wriggling in ecstasy. Ray sucked her nipples passionately while his hand caressed the moistness between her legs through her pants. He squeezed her buttocks and pulled down her miniskirt along with her panty. Kimaya twisted and adjusted her long legs to quickly slide down the coiled panty.

"I want you inside me," she said softly in his ears. Ray pulled down his shorts with one hand while his other arm jammed Kimaya's hand over her head. His tongue continued to tease her nipple. Kimaya groaned and whimpered.

Without wavering from the eye contact, she lifted her legs to clasp him around his waist. Balancing on one elbow, Ray took his pulsating manhood and aimed straight at the sweet spot between her legs. "It's tight," he breathed heavily. Kimaya's eyes were shut as she waited anxiously for the burning organ that would quench the fire raging inside her. It was happening exactly as she had fantasized.

"Let me guide it," she moaned, unable to control herself and shoved her arm between her legs to encircle his penis. She slightly tightened her grip to feel the hardness. Then she gently scratched it along the length with her nails, playing with it.

"Don't! Wait!" he panicked and grabbed her wrist. But it was too late. A spurt of hot sticky fluid pinched her thighs as the fascinating organ between her slender fingers rocked as if in a fit. Ray groaned in her ears, his sweaty body stretched to welcome the orgasm. He slumped over her after the euphoria and spasm subsided, dropping his head into the pillow beside her.

"What happened?" she asked innocently as she felt his body turning cold and the enchanting piece lifeless.

He was breathless. He did not answer.

Ray lay wide-awake on the sofa. He had not blinked the entire night. He squinted at the wall clock across the room. Four-thirty, it declared. More than thirty years had passed since that tumultuous evening, thirty-three to be exact. The memory was buried deep in an unfathomable abyss, not to be peeked ever. He did not find any reason to disclose it to Tina at any point after their marriage. Whatever happened before they took the vows was something very personal to him or her, he reasoned.

But things were a little different now, he thought. His soul mate had to be brought into confidence regarding the chaos and turmoil that was pushing him to the brink. He didn't have much time to consider his options.

He pushed away the sheet, brought in a pen and paper and started writing.

It was tiring and laborious for he had always been unnerved to take a glimpse into his childhood with Kimaya. After two hours, holding the paper in front, he felt lively, spirited and nervous like an excited inexperienced pilot on his first flight. After years he felt like going for a jog.

He neatly folded the letter, put it safely inside his personal drawer, took a deep breath and reached for his sneakers.

Tina did not speak for a long time. The letter dangled from her fingers as she slouched on the sofa at one corner. Ray sat facing her at the other end. Kids were in school. Ray tried to read her thoughts as she stared blankly as if in deep contemplation, but could not come to any definite conclusion. Are her eyes moist? He was not sure.

"Why this letter?" "You could have just told me about it." Tina wondered aloud.

"I didn't want to overlook anything. You had to know our background, our deep bond, everything. Moreover, I don't think I have the courage to say it directly, so writing it down is easier," Ray added softly.

"I know you guys were once great friends. In the last fifteen years, I have hung out with Kimaya more than you have. She had told me how, as kids, you two were glued to each other. How your classmates would jeer at you for being her devotee. "I still don't see the point of... this letter," she reflected.

"You don't get it. That evening crushed everything," he said softly, looking down at the carpet as if choosing every word.

"I get it. You had sex at sixteen or seventeen, or rather, you tried to, and it was definitely scandalous thirty years ago, but now I am not so sure. "Kids wouldn't think twice about it these days," she joked. "Is that what you are saying?" she asked.

"No. I lost my best friend that day. I lost the woman I adored that day," he was having difficulty uttering each word and was barely audible.

"How?" she asked, scratching her head.

"I failed her. I failed the woman who was always there for me, who would risk anything for me. I was not good enough for her," he noticed the lump rising up his throat. A thin layer of wetness covered his eyes.

"It is all right. What happened was perfectly natural and common," she said confidently as if she were privy to several such experiences. "That's what I have heard," she quickly added.

"I know but that evening something snapped inside me. I was riddled with guilt and shame that I was not worthy of her. My brain would explode as images of those final moments played out constantly in my head. I wished I could turn the clock back and reenact, replay the whole evening as I had envisioned it countless times," his lips quivered as he spoke. "I could not get over it."

Tina sat, mesmerized as her husband bared it all for the first time. This was a new man.

"I shunned her out of my life. I started avoiding her. I always had excuses not to see her when earlier I would dig for reasons to meet her. I was embarrassed to face her, to look into her eyes when she would come over as if nothing had happened. I was scared that I might again disappoint her", a drop took shape at his lower eyelids, dropped on his blue denim and dispersed to form a wide blotch.

"I threw her out of my life without any fault of hers. I disappointed her, not only that evening, but forever after that," he immersed his face in his palms and sobbed as flood of tears escaped his eye like an unruly river.

Tina came near, put her arms on his shoulders and gently massaged it. Ray wept inconsolably; the knots that had chained his consciousness for more than thirty years were being untied.

Ray remained buried, long after the sobs had subsided. He took the hand towel that Tina had unsuccessfully tried to push into his hands, wiped his face and turned to face her with reddened eyes. He managed a quivering smile while she massaged her neck and shoulders.

"But…" she hesitated after Ray appeared stable.

"I know what you are thinking," he had regained his composure. "Why have I recently started… blatantly…. touching her?"

Tina nodded

"I don't really know," he offered.

Tina was obviously not satisfied. She gave him a questioning look.

"Our friendship declined after that day due to my guilt and shame." We had not spoken or acknowledged each other in school or around the neighbourhood for months. Our parents and friends were bewildered, but none directly confronted us. We were in different colleges a year later. I was in a boarding in Delhi while she joined a college in Kolkata. I later heard from one of our common friends that she got married to a guy from her college. Several years later, I got married. "Come to think of it, I married late," he smiled.

She smiled back.

"One year after our wedding when she came with her kids to stay with her parents, due to her husband's tragic death, I was seeing her after more than a decade. And in the last fifteen years, she has grown closer to you than me. With caution, we became amiable over the years, as it was difficult to avoid her or maybe I didn't want to anymore. But we always felt a restrained, maybe it was my creation" he put his hand on hers.

"And like a coward, as I always have been when it comes to her, I was never able to muster the nerve to face her…to tell her I was sorry for deserting her; for hurting her," Ray said sadly. "I wish she would just slap me or scold me for being impertinent or shameless or would rudely shrug my hand off her thighs to show her disapproval. But we know that she has always been brave and mature. She still is," his eyes became moist again. "But time is running out."

"For what?" she frowned.

"For me to ask for forgiveness and hurting her; for breaking her heart; for being foolish; for snubbing a valuable friend," he said philosophically.

"What do you mean?" she asked without batting an eyelid.

"She is suffering from throat cancer; advanced stage. Her days are numbered," he said softly.

"What?" she gasped. "When? How?"

"Only Nikki knows. She told me a month back. Kimaya has not disclosed it to Deb. It would shatter her, she says. She worships her brave mother," said Ray.

"What?" Tina was still in denial. It was difficult to grasp. Kimaya was suffering from cancer…unimaginable.

"You have to go now, before it is too late," she demanded.

"I will," he said.

Despite the grim prognosis delivered by a team of doctors, Kimaya made the bold decision to decline chemotherapy. With the disease in its final stages and spreading rapidly, she resolved to live the rest of her days on her own terms, free from the agony of painful treatments and futile medications. She was determined to make every moment count, embracing her fate with grace and dignity.

However, as the pain intensified and her condition worsened, Kimaya's daughters had no choice but to call for an ambulance.

Ray and Tina made a steadfast commitment to visit her every day at the hospital. Though it pained them to see their dear friend in such agony, they stood by her side, offering comfort and support as best they could.

"Where is Tina?" she gestured with her lips and eyes. Tracheostomy, a procedure to connect the ventilator to the throat for forced respiration, had killed her voice. Ray's eyes would well up whenever he entered her isolated chamber.

"She is on her way," he said.

Kimaya smiled.

"Can I have a minute alone?" he looked at Nikki.

"Sure Uncle," she said.

Ray pulled his chair near the bed and softly caressed her forehead. Their eyes locked like it did in that magical moment more than thirty years back. She was still ravishing; her long tresses flowed to the sides like undulating waves flowing in a calm ocean. And then their eyes talked clearly as it did once.

'*Are you sure?*' it said

'*Yes,*' said the other.

Gently he brought his lips to touch hers.

Tears flowed like a heavy downpour, soaking her soft pillow.

She had longed and dreamt the moment for thirty-three years.

The wait was over.

The Instinctive Couple

"These elaborate ceremonies are such a waste of time and money," yawned Aman.

"I always wanted my wedding to be an elaborate affair. That is how we grew up; grand decorations, the bustle of feisty relatives, ornate makeups and endless ceremonies. Oh! I love it. I wish the dream would never end," Simran was wide-awake. It was three AM in the morning. She tied her long black hair into a knot while pulling herself up against the headboard.

"Can we sleep?" Aman yawned again.

"They say once the couple gets married these endless nights of chatting are over," she continued, ignoring Aman's plea.

"Obviously. Once they start living together, they can talk directly," he mocked jokingly.

"Very funny. But I find our long chats very romantic especially when they last till early hours of the morning. It makes me feel connected, as if we can speak at length about anything but you seem so disinterested," she signed, caressing her long hair. Her straight hair touched her waist when she stood tall at five feet seven inches. Simran had big eyes with a prominent nose, pouty lips and her fair skin was unblemished like a baby's. When she smiled, her cheeks curved deep to reveal the most prominent pair of dimples.

"And moreover, once married, nights are for taking care of a more serious affair, which entails minimal talking," said Aman lazily, stretching his body.

"You boys have only one thing in your head," smiled Simran into the phone that lay on the duvet. She had switched on the phone speakers to relax her arms that ached from being attached to her ears for hours.

"Are you not dreaming of sweaty nights full of passion and love?" smiled Aman, his energy miraculously resurfacing. At six feet, Aman's heavy frame, covered mostly with fat, was reminiscent of the time during his college days when he used to be a regular at the local gym. Any offhand observer would dismiss him as a typical unhealthy Delhi businessman. His father on the other hand would, at slightest opportunity, proudly laud his son's academic achievements, the first lad in their family with an Engineering degree. Aman possessed an amiable demeanor and a reserved nature.

"I love the *Sangeet* ceremony that commences tomorrow and my dad wants it to continue for a week till the day before our wedding," said Simran, evading his favourite topic.

"You did not answer my question," Aman was adamant.

"My friends are completely geared up to tease you," giggled Simran

"We are also not going to take things lying down," countered Aman, giving up on his earlier interest.

"Please don't mind if at times you get hit below the belt. Ok? My friends can be nasty if they so decide," said Simran

"Don't worry Simran. It's all for fun and I am sure your friends are mature enough to understand if any risqué flier comes their way," said Aman reassuringly.

"My friends are a coolest lot," Simran defended, "They are looking forward to see you tomorrow,"

"My battery is about to conk off. Another four percent remaining," Aman peered at the screen. "It's almost four in the morning," he shrieked, outraged.

"Is my baby sleepy?" sang Simran.

"Yes, my mother, since a long time," Aman responded in the same tone. "Let's get some sleep, Simran," continued Aman earnestly, "it is going to be a long and an exciting day tomorrow…I mean today."

"Okay. Sleep well, my baby. See you today," cooed Simran.

"Good night…or rather good morning. See you later," said Aman gently before tossing the phone on the side table and pulling the quilt over his head.

Mr. Harjeet Singh, at six feet with a straight posture and heavy build was an imposing person. His stern expressionless face masked his soft heart while his discerning mind, sharpened through years of experience possessed a unique ability to pierce through any peculiarity. He had worked hard all his life to set up a flourishing business. He owned several shops dealing in electrical equipment in upscale markets all over Delhi.

Harjeet had expressed his reservations for the nuptials when Simran had brought Aman to their house for the first time.

"I don't think he is the right partner for you," he bared after Aman had left.

"Why?" Simran was ready for the argument as if she was expecting his opening line.

"I don't know exactly, but he comes across as shrewd and selfish.... not refined," he pondered.

"But Dad, you just met him for the first time!" exclaimed Simran.

"And how long have you known him?" Mr. Singh tossed aside the newspaper, which was lying on his lap and stared straight at his daughter.

"Six months," Simran shook her head.

"And you think six months is enough to know all the eccentricities in a person. Even after being married to your mother for thirty years, I sometimes get a feeling that I hardly know her," he winked at Arpita, who glared back, *"And you are sure of Aman the great in six months."*

"But your hunch can be misplaced. Who doesn't have weaknesses, dad? And by your own admission about Mom, one could scrape for thirty years and still be unsure," Simran tried hard to wash the caustic tone from her voice but failed. She was getting edgy. She looked away.

"There are thousands of prospective grooms in dozens of online matrimonial portals who would barter a hand to get married to a beautiful girl like you. What I am suggesting is to go a bit slow on Aman and explore a few more eligible boys," said Harjeet, leaning back on the sofa. He glanced at Arpita to elicit an approval for his point of view, but received a blank expression.

"What do you mean by 'go slow on Aman'? He is not some stock option we are mulling that we can 'go slow'. I will have to completely reject him before looking elsewhere. We have been talking every day for the past six months; I know him and we have promised a world of happiness to each other," concluded Simran, making herself comfortable on the settee.

Knowing his daughter, Harjeet was aware that what he was trying to achieve was far-fetched, but in the least, he wanted to put forth his point. And when the head is hazy with foggy clouds of love, one cannot see beyond, he rued. He was risking being his daughter's sole adversary in the whole affair, but then it was her life that was at stake, and he could not let her go without revealing his heart.

"You found Aman through a marriage website. All I am asking of you is to reconsider your engagement with him because it would kill me to see your heart broken and you know that. After the initial euphoria of marriage subsides, and it will, mundane routines take over and marriage may seem difficult or strenuous at times. In those moments, real strength of character is tested. Whether Aman can weather the storm and ride you both to safety enduringly, I don't know but I hope you have made the right choice," Harjeet looked away lest Simran should notice his glistening eyes.

Simran came and sat in between her parents, closer to her father. She slid her arm to clasp her father's palm.

"I know you are always there Dad; maybe it is that sense of security which pushes me to unchartered territories without fear. Don't nourish any apprehension about Aman, he may appear a little queer or socially reticent but he is a good person at heart," said Simran, pushing herself closer to her father.

Harjeet put his right hand over his daughter's thin shoulders and pulled her in a light embrace.

"Thank God it's D-Day tomorrow. We would have been scuba diving in Thailand if you had agreed to a court marriage, as I had suggested," said Aman, pinning the phone to his ear with his shoulder as he stumbled on one leg to put on a pair of pajamas.

"Oh! I loved every moment. My dad took extra pain to accommodate even our distant relatives, whom we had not met in two decades. Last week just flew by in a flash, singing, dancing, connecting – so much energy. It was the longest party of my life," said Simran, getting inside her soft quilt.

"Your dad seems sort of orthodox.... the strict type," said Aman, comfortably snuggled inside the thick quilt.

"For certain things." said Simran, "He considers marriage a holy alliance; made in heaven. Right? He believes that all rituals are holy, approved by our ancestors with the consent of the almighty and hence imperative. Blessings from our forefathers is vital for our happiness together and for that the rules have to be followed," explained Simran.

"I hope the ritual pressure won't continue after tomorrow?" said Aman.

"I am sure your relatives too must be celebrating," wondered Simran

"My father is not the pious variety. His business is his world. My Mom is taking care of all the arrangements, which I must add, in no way matches your Dad's commitment to details," clarified Aman

"Did you ever imagine going in for an arranged marriage, that too through an online portal?" asked Simran, turning to one side, her phone glued to her ear.

"No one was falling in love with me," lamented Aman playfully.

"I hope we are making the correct decision," Simran stiffened.

"We are getting married tomorrow Simran. Are you having doubts?" Aman lifted himself to rest against a raised pillow.

"I love you Aman and want to spend my remaining days taking care of our nest. I wanted to know if you are sure about us?" asked Simran softly.

"Don't be anxious, Simran. It is normal, I guess, to experience some uneasiness before taking the plunge but rest assured. We will have a great time together. There is no doubt today that I want to marry you," said Aman with finality.

"I wonder if you have trimmed the extra hair poking out through your nostrils that I pointed out to you during the *Sangeet* at our place. Trim it before the wedding tomorrow, it looks repulsive," said Simran seriously.

"Yes, my Lady. Anything else?"

"See you tomorrow, my love," smiled Simran affectionately.

"Good night dear," said Aman and hung up.

The wedding sailed through smoothly riding on excellent arrangement and management by Harjeet. Key areas, such as receiving the groom's entourage, making several hundred guests comfortable, arrangement and service of starters and food, decoration of the actual seat for tying the knot in front of the fire on an embellished platform, taking care of the bride, overseeing the prompt and efficient parking of the incessant flow of cars, etc. were meticulously identified by Harjeet and supervision delegated to responsible members of the family.

Though the young blood in the family vied for the key and delectable responsibility of controlling the bar, the responsibility eventually landed on the shoulders of Surjeet, Simran's far cousin. Surjeet stood behind the wooden counter hurling expletives at his tipsy cousins with increasing frequency.

Simran looked breathtaking in an ornate maroon bridal wear, her face made up in detail during the three hour sitting at an upscale parlour. Sitting beside her, Aman appeared strikingly lackluster; the fancy embroidered blue and golden *Sherwani* was the sole saving grace.

A week's honeymoon in Thailand was over before the couple could think of sincerely exploring the place. Like a new toy in a child's hand, they struggled to keep their hands off each other. The passion for each other and the uninhibited energy surprised them at times.

Strangely, a simple declaration of union by an undistinguished Priest, as accepted by all cultures worldwide, could break the chains of coyness to unleash the suppressed fire and spur us for unrestrained manifestation of love.

They felt an indescribable heavenly connection.

As planned, upon their return from Thailand, the couple shifted to Pune. Aman had landed himself a lucrative promotion as Project head in a relatively smaller IT firm headquartered at the IT Park in Pune - a booming township, teeming with professionals. Most of the major IT companies in the country had rushed to open their regional offices in the area prompting a surge in real estate activities.

The couple rented a modest two-bedroom apartment in the area.

Things settled into a routine.

Though Simran was qualified and competent with a Masters degree under her belt, she chose to take care of their love nest and keep it immaculate. 'I don't want you to work', Aman had said when they were dating and promised to keep her like a queen. Simran had agreed, as she imagined herself on her toes with two, maybe three cuties pulling at her from all angles. She loved children.

Simran engaged herself with household chores, packed lunch for Aman and frequently looked up new recipes for dinner. But mostly, particularly during the afternoon she found herself unoccupied and listless as she despised watching TV or reading. Frequently hitting the market or mall alone to window-shop did not fascinate her. New acquaintances had to be created in the neighbourhood, she reflected.

Boredom was stealthily creeping in along with an unknown feeling of confinement or rather dependence. If Aman is not excited to have a child immediately, she might as well start working, she thought.

The new promotion kept Aman occupied. He got entrapped in eternally striving to get better, brighter and being 'more' productive for 'better' survival. On normal days he would leave his office for home after nine in the evening. He would grab a bunch of roses or a bouquet from the flower vendor below his office for Simran on his way back. Sundays were eagerly awaited by both for distinctly opposite reasons; for one to be out of the house with Aman after breakfast and for the other to sleep through the day. Aman would laboriously pull and push himself to wander the streets of Pune.

Simran was in no hurry to divulge her desire to get an occupation; at times she indulged herself with indolence or listened to solitude. Couple of months' delay would not shake the earth, she reasoned.

Six months flew by before the fateful day arrived.

"Cappuccino," said Aman, keeping the menu down. He rubbed his cheeks to feel his stubble. He made a mental note to shave before he went to bed.

The day had begun lazily like any other Sunday as if the mind and body were in collusion to resist any display of exuberance or spirit. The sloth would be further exacerbated by late night passion, flow of adrenalin and blend of hormones; all dancing in unison to explode into a climax that left the couple blissfully enervated.

"Anything to munch?" asked Simran as she rose to place their order at the counter. She wore a long floral skirt in yellow with an orange figure-hugging top and an eye-catching white stone necklace.

Aman nodded sideways. The Bean King, their regular hangout for an evening coffee on Sundays was teeming with aficionados from all ages but young couples clearly outnumbered any other combinations of companionship.

Aman fidgeted with his mobile, half-heartedly opened his mail box for any new mail and on finding none, exited it swiftly as he waited at the secluded corner. The round table for two and the comfortable metal chairs fitted with hard cushions was to the left of the main glass entrance door, away from the open floor of the restaurant. It was sort of a semi-private enclosure flanked by two big pillars that separated it from the main area.

Aman had no reason to be alarmed or threatened. People wore dark glasses everywhere these days, nothing curious about that in a coffee shop. The lanky guy in blue denim and loose white t-shirt seemed…. normal, but then their moment together was fleeting for him to even speculate. The guy had vanished long before Aman opened the note that he had placed firmly on the table.

"She does not love you."

Aman twiddled with the note, flipping it over to unearth any more clues to the one-liner that had jolted him out of his reverie. He sat up straight to stretch his neck all–around to suspiciously scrutinize every face. The devotees of the popular joint were engaged in animated or silent conversation while some were immersed in their laptop. Their ignorance of the turbulence brewing in the corner joined them with a common thread.

"She does not love you," muttered Aman softly under his breath.

"She does not love you," he repeated, staring at the note, wet with sweat from his palms.

The blue ball pen ink on a soft white tissue paper was prominent, the 'not' in the centre of the short sentence was emboldened with several strokes. Aman could not get his eyes off that word.

"That queue was endless. Are you ok?" asked Simran as she pulled the chair and sat down.

"Yeah," uttered Aman weakly.

"You are sweating like crazy," said Simran as she stretched to wipe the beads of sweat lined on Aman's forehead with her pink hand towel. Aman blocked her arm, swaying his head away like a boxer sparring to foil a jab.

"What is the matter with you," Simran frowned, her patience falling apart, "you were fine a couple of minutes ago when I left you and now you appear as though you saw the devil enter the coffee shop."

"What?" Aman was not listening. His face had turned ashen, forehead and neck wet with the flowing sweat. His mind was on an uncontrollable rampage like a wild elephant on a riot. He looked up at Simran as if she were a stranger.

The couple noticed the waiter standing over them with their order when he finally grunted to draw their attention. His arms were paining from holding the tray.

As Aman rose without looking up, the metal chair fell back with a sharp clink, drawing several heads towards him. The waiter jumped to pick the fallen chair as Simran stared at Aman, perplexed and shocked. He strode purposefully to the exit and was gone.

When several calls to Aman went unanswered, Simran picked up her bag and left the café.

The coffee remained untouched.

"What is wrong with you?" Simran demanded, almost teary eyed. Aman was sitting on the sofa, his legs on the centre table. She had rushed from the café to their apartment with her set of keys dangling from her fingers all the way.

Aman was still uncommunicative, his body exuding disquiet, his expression harsh and fingers coiled tightly into a fist. He looked up briefly to meet Simran's miserable eyes and went back to his world.

"Are you going to speak or what?" yelled Simran, her patience busted.

She came and sat beside him and placed her arm on his shoulder. An inexplicable fear, that she hardly knew the person she was married to was slowly firming inside her as she tried to unravel Aman's mysterious behaviour. Aman fidgeted as if Simran's arm was a giant leech sucking on his shoulders. He shrugged off her arm and shifted to a corner to face her, his face tense with anguish.

"How many boyfriends did you have before we got married?" scoffed Aman. He trembled as he spoke.

"What kind of question is that?" frowned Simran.

"You don't like the question?" Aman was getting charged.

"Why is it suddenly so relevant?? We had agreed to keep the topic out of our radar," Simran was livid.

"So let me rephrase it to a suitable question; do you have a boyfriend…now?" Aman had been boiling for quite some time and his words hit Simran like burning embers.

"What?" Simran barked.

"You heard me," he glared.

"I have never seen you like this. What has gotten into you? Why are you hell bent on ruining the day?" Simran softened a decibel.

"Ruining the day! My life is ruined," came the crisp retort as Aman shoved the crumpled tissue paper into her thin hands.

"Who gave you this?" Simran looked up.

"You tell me," mocked Aman

"I don't have a clue," said Simran, flipping the paper.

"Don't lie to me. What have you been up to when I was slogging my ass off for us in the office?" he shouted.

"You are making me sick, Aman. You have no right to accuse me with such repulsive allegations when you don't have any concrete evidence." she yelled back.

"The proof is in your hands," said Aman, pointing at her clasped palm.

"How can you believe something so sketchy… unconvincing? What about the relationship we have…the trust …the connection…Don't you know me Aman?" Simran was out of breath, trying hard for a breakthrough.

"Maybe I don't know you…maybe it was all a sham?" came the rejoinder

"What nonsense," she was getting frustrated, "why would I get married to you if there were someone else? My father had not put a gun on my temple or traded me for pots of gold that I had no choice. On the contrary he had urged me to be absolutely clear about you," she reasoned. "Maybe he was right," she had not wanted to say it, but then things were not under her control.

"Does it make any sense to you?" she said, lifting the crumpled tissue paper.

"I don't know. What I know is that some fair guy with large sunglasses put that paper in my hand and broke the fake dream I was living. That is what I know," he replied with conviction.

"Maybe it was meant for someone else," Simran raised an eyebrow.

"Do you think it is usual for married couples, once in a while, to get hit by a random paper dart, meant for someone else? That's highly unlikely. The blessed paper was meant for me and it says that you don't love me," Aman was shaking.

"And you believe it like a heavenly gospel?" asked Simran with pursed lips.

"For a moment even if I yield to your innocence, the fact still remains that someone is out there stalking us…. you to be precise, maybe from the moment we arrived here. And he means business. There can be no smoke without a fire burning somewhere; a guy from your past is fired up to track you down…and the instant that fire reignites in you and it eventually will, it will smother me with the smoke in its wake. That is what I believe and I am not willing to take things lying down," Aman was clear and emphatic.

"What do you want, Aman? Don't do this to us. There is no guy. There is no one. There is only you and that is the truth," said Simran, almost on the verge of breaking down, the flood of tears longing to gush out.

"I have made up my mind. I need a drink," Aman was out of the apartment like a bullet.

The night was going to be a long one. Simran let the tears flow uncontrollably.

"Who is that guy?" asked Monica

"Guy?" her forehead crinkled.

"He is forever staring at you," said Monica, pinching her arm.

"Stop it! There is hardly any place to move. And the bus is crammed with guys staring all over. So stop imagining things," she nudged with her elbow.

"He is there every day from the University to our stop. He never sits down or smiles," declared Monica

"Do you love that boy?" asked a grave voice

"Dad!" she shrieked.

"Uncle!" gasped Monica.

"Don't marry that guy?" he said seriously.

"Which guy dad? What are you saying?" she pleaded.

"He is not good enough for you. Don't marry him," he repeated.

"There is no guy dad. What is the matter with both of you," she looked from one to the other.

"Don't waste your life. Don't marry him," he started singing.

"There is no guy," the scream rattled her ears as she jerked upright, her arms stretched in tension, palms squeezing the sheets.

The heavy breathing gradually receded. Simran remained transfixed in that position for several minutes while her dazed eyes gradually adjusted to the dull light.

Aman had not returned the previous night by the time she had dozed off.

Shades were still drawn, rather unprecedented, as Aman, an early riser, would normally attend to them upon leaving the bed. Simran noticed that the pillows on his side lay untouched. Disoriented cushions on the sofa and an empty beer bottle on the floor told another story. He had left without a word or breakfast.

A piercing headache gripped her on the right side while her stomach, without food since the previous afternoon, churned menacingly.

She will call him later; she thought and trudged to the bathroom.

"Have you seen my mobile?" asked Simran.

Aman had changed into casuals after returning from office. He sat comfortably on the sofa with a half filled beer mug on one hand and the TV remote on the other. Sensing an inhibition to talk, Simran had remained out of his way for most of the evening, but that could not go on forever. And what about beer? Maybe he will stop once our little tiff is over. So every time we quarrel, he would drink like a fish or what, wondered Simran. But then this was no ordinary fight, she reminded herself.

"I wanted to call you in the morning, but couldn't find the damn phone," Simran sat on the adjacent sofa.

"Why did you want to call me?" The sarcasm was obvious.

"To speak with you," Simran struggled to sound calm.

"Or maybe to speak with your boyfriend," Aman mocked, tapping his curved index fingers in the air to depict inverted commas.

"I don't want the evening to be a repetition of yesterday. Have you seen my phone?" she asked again.

"I threw it from our balcony this morning," said Aman, taking a sip from his mug.

"What?" her voice choked with shock.

"See, how desperate you sound… to speak to your lover…see…you bitch! I will not let that happen. Who knows; maybe it was your idea to drop that note at the café, no wonder you took so long to order two coffees," Aman was unstoppable.

"How can you throw my phone away? Are you out of your mind?" asked Simran, hopelessly scandalized.

"I can do anything," said Aman with bitterness.

"Please don't do this to us, Aman. I beg of you," she pleaded with teary eyes.

"Bitch,"

The word continued to strike her head like a blacksmith's hammer persistently pounding his piece on the anvil. She felt feeble, drained and scared. Who was this stranger in her house? Thin streams of tears rolled down her pink cheeks with effortless ease.

Aman raised the volume to drown the muffled sobs.

"Is the guy wearing dark sunglasses?" she was nervous

"It's definitely not light ones," said Monica

"Is he the thin type?" she asked, glancing furtively

"Looks thin," squinted Monica

"Is he carrying a tissue paper?" she asked anxiously

"He is waving something white," said Monica

"I wonder if he likes coffee," she smiled

"Don't marry that guy," he said

"I am not marrying anyone, Dad," she said

"You should ask him for coffee," said Monica.

"You think so? She wondered.

"He threw a tissue paper at us. What impudence! What has he scribbled on it?"

"It says he loves you," smiled Monica.

"Don't marry!" he said.

"Dad!"

The slamming of the door brought her back to the dark and dreary room. Aman had left again without a word. She slumped back into the soft pillow and stared at the fancy ceiling, her eyes wide open. The drapes were still in place, blocking the sun. And what is it with these crazy dreams? I am going insane, she thought. The back of her head ached and her eyes burnt from the disturbed sleep.

I need some fresh air, she reflected as she tugged the drapes to one corner, soaking the room with light.

The empty key holder near the exit door felt like a bolt from the blue. She stumbled to the nearest chair as her knees shook with weakness. To discover that her house keys were missing from their place after having painstakingly dressed for an outside lunch made her furious. *'How could Aman stoop so low?'*

She remained on the chair for what seemed like a century; anger, frustration and dread – a cocktail of emotions pervaded every cell of her body.

Couple of hours later, the fire alarm resonated through the entire compound.

As the narration progressed, her manner shifted from impatience to calm, from high-pitched breathlessness to a relaxed countenance, from hesitation to indifference. An eerie silence gripped the living room as Simran finished recounting the sudden turn of events of the past few days. Arpita looked shocked and sad, Harjeet livid while Monica, her only confidante since school, concerned and sympathetic.

"How did you escape…I mean get out?" Monica finally broke the silence. Sensing something was amiss she had hastily arranged for Simran's flight to Delhi, but what she was hearing was something entirely unimaginable.

"I put a light near one of the sprinkler heads in the living room, triggering the system. The rest followed automatically. Someone rushed inside in a matter of minutes using the master key," Simran explained.

"I will kill that bastard. How dare he treat you like that? I always found him…abnormal. I knew he would be the first to run if thieves entered the house," Harjeet barked. The erstwhile prejudice rose instantly like helium filled balloons.

"What now?" Arpita was apprehensive.

"I don't know," Simran shook her head

"What is there to know? We are done with that son of a…Can any person with a decent upbringing stoop so low.

Anything could have happened; what if she suddenly felt sick – without a phone… locked inside… God!" puffed Harjeet.

"But…" Arpita was worried.

Harjeet raised his hand to crush any opposing views.

"Speak with him once. That's the tenth time he has called since morning," said Arpita, putting down the receiver.

"I don't want to talk, Mama," said Simran.

"Your mother and I were thinking…. that," faltered Harjeet as if he were learning to speak.

Simran raised an eyebrow. Her father's uncomfortable tone was uncommon. She waited.

"Do you…you know…have a…you know…" he stared at his wife for support.

"…Have a friend…?" Arpita completed the sentence, much to his relief. The omitted prefix before 'friend' made it more evident.

"What?" she heard it but couldn't believe her parents were singing Aman's tune within a couple of days.

"We mean if you have one…it's perfectly all right…that's your choice. We only have your well-being at heart," Harjeet defended.

"Why would anyone drop a note for no reason?" Arpita asked, facing her husband.

What wrong Aman committed if her own parents were capable of pointing a finger at her and question her credibility, she thought.

"How can you even imagine that," Simran raised her voice.

"What if someone from your past still nurtures a desire for you? … Karan…?" he whispered.

"What Karan?" Simran was totally agitated and disgusted. "You don't have a clue but would not refrain from divulging your uncontrolled imagination. We parted three years ago and he is in the US…married, for heaven's sake."

"But the note…" Harjeet was desperate to be convinced that his daughter was unblemished. He did not care about Aman, but he had to be absolutely certain about his daughter, certain that his social reputation was not at risk of being undermined.

"What about the note? Why don't you find out? Maybe it was a waiter in the coffee shop, maybe a neighbour from our building, or maybe someone from my past. Who cares? I don't want to know because I am not interested. I know where I stand. I know that Aman has broken the trust. And you guys are making me sick," snubbed Simran.

"If you think the relationship is unworkable, make it absolutely clear to him," reasoned Arpita, realizing that their conversation was over.

"I will. It's only the second day since I left him. Give me some time," said Simran and left her parents to stare at each other.

"I love you," purred Aman

"I love you, Simran," he repeated when met with silence.

"Please come back," he pleaded

"Stop it," she couldn't hold it any further. Continuous ringing of the landline through the day had forced Harjeet to request her daughter to talk.

"How could you leave me like that? You know I love you," said Aman.

"And how could you lock me and throw my phone away?" retorted Simran.

"I had not thrown your mobile. It's lying in my bag," said Aman weakly.

"Whatever. It's one and the same thing. For me it's as good as thrown away. And on top of that you had the audacity to lock me inside. I am not an ignorant illiterate, who would be steamrolled into submission," Simran was furious.

"I have apologized to your parents whenever your mother had picked up the phone and I am telling you – I am sorry…very sorry for being an ass," his voice trembled.

"The real point is not the phone…. it's that you don't trust me anymore. The seed of suspicion is now sown and there can never be a worthy relationship without trust," she said

"How do you know that the seed of suspicion is unshakable?" asked Aman

"Well that's the clear message I got from you. You claimed that our life together was as good as over. You were absolutely convinced that I was…cheating…that I was a…" she could not complete the sentence.

"I am willing to trust you. I have faith in you. Please come back," he entreated, not really caring for what she said.

"Maybe I don't trust you anymore. Maybe I don't feel safe with you. Maybe you scare me. Maybe we were not supposed to be together," she was almost inaudible.

"I will not question your frame of mind or the resentment; it's understandable. When I returned early from office that day, filled with guilt for taking your keys and tiptoed inside the drenched and slippery apartment, the only missing valuable was you. That moment I realized what a fool I had been and what immense significance you hold for me," lamented Aman.

"That is no way to treat that which is so valuable," said Simran. She had vowed not to cry in front of him again, but that resolve was getting weakened.

"I know. I made a blunder. I am not perfect but I am willing to learn, to change," he said resolutely.

"All that is fine, Aman," she took her name for the first time, "but I am wholly shaken by your conduct. I feel you are capable of inflicting serious harm or physical abuse," Simran hesitated.

"Did I do anything of that nature? How do you know that for sure? Even though I was dead drunk for two nights, I kept my distance. I know where to draw the line," Aman was offended.

"What is the guarantee that such behavior will not be repeated in the future?" she asked.

"To be honest there is no guarantee," Aman was direct.

The intermittent hiss of their breath resonated through what seemed an eternal silence. Simran broke it first, "I am…not sure Aman…I don't know…Let me…"

"You want me to say that henceforth I would be a perfect husband. That would be a lie. I don't know how I would be. What I know is that I won't let you go again," Aman was calm.

"But you scared me Aman…."

"How would you have reacted if, on that ill-omened day, an attractive women had approached you, looked you in the eye and declared; 'he doesn't love you."

Mind, they say, is capable of reaching the fringes of the universe in a fraction of seconds. Such is the speed of its travel.

Aman's sudden charge led straight to the visualization of a pretty lady in his strong arms. It sucked the breath out of her lungs. Her eyes narrowed to an intense gaze as the figures in front of her eyes took shape and a passionate movie started playing automatically, without her control. A rapid series of images whirled on her mind's giant screen, that created a storm within her, turbulence so wild that it numbed her sense of reasoning. And then she found herself in the drama, transformed into a spirit so malicious that she gasped at its sight. In a flash, from a girl next door, she was filled with an overpowering retributive hatred. The loving couple lay before her, writhing in pain, choking in their blood.

She saw herself without any qualm, justifying the massacre as a thin line of blood trickled down the blade of the hatchet in her hand.

She did not notice when the receiver slipped out of her soft fingers. She sat down on the edge of the bed, shaking nervously. She was going to be sick.

"I will start applying for a job from tomorrow," she said as they relaxed in the living room, sipping the tea prepared by Aman. Her suitcase lay unopened at a distance.

Harjeet, as always, yielded, once she had made the decision. He showered his abundant blessings.

Aman pulled her close and pushed his lips on hers. With their eyes shut, their tongues greeted each other.

"No, I am serious," she smiled, once they broke away from the protracted kissing.

"Let's go to the bedroom," smiled Aman, kissing her neck.

"Aman!"

"And don't lock me inside if you leave early for work," he whispered in her ears.

The Hazy Sunrise

"Ronny! We don't have whole day!" barked Mrs. Jones hurling the whiteboard marker's black cap towards him. She made no attempt to conceal her exasperation.

Ronny stood poker-faced as he imagined himself flapping his giant wings out in the sky or aliens suddenly entering the room to proclaim him as their leader, relieving him of the ordeal.

He could overhear a muffled giggle nearby; it must be Raj, the dimwit, concluded Ronny.

"What is the matter, Ronny?" Mrs. Jones was struggling to be calm, "We know you are a diligent and an industrious lad; teachers are fond of you but this is English pronunciation class where you have to read aloud and I see that you are always blank. It is stark impudence and disrespect," she paused for breath.

Ronny opened his palm and offered the pen cap, which he had immediately picked up when struck. He hoped it might give him some points, however inconsequential.

"Is this attitude going to help?" she demanded rhetorically.

Ronny didn't offer any explanation. He stood with his head bowed.

"I reckon a meeting with your parents can throw some light. Lindy, you read from the board," she said, moving towards it.

That was the last thing Ronny would have been enthusiastic about. He shuddered at the thought of being together with his parents inside the Principal's chamber.

"And you - keep standing," she pointed sternly at Ronny.

"Are you alright?" squinted Mrs. Xavier

"I am fine," said Ronny, slowly stretching his lips to a smile.

"But you look pale, don't lie to your Mom," said Rose pulling him closer.

Ronny briefly looked in her eyes and pulled away, throwing himself on the couch opposite to her. With a straight face he waited for her to goad while his blue eyes revealed zilch. Ronny was a plump lad with thick straight hair; his round cheeks often enticed elders to pinch them as a show of adoration. He was that rare breed of students who are passionate about books and possess a feisty desire to learn. He had to be threatened to go out and play.

Rose did not push further, dismissing the issue as nickel-and-dime. Ronny, being hard working and bright, seldom gave her reasons for concern on the school front.

"Are you hungry?" the doting mother was back.

"Not really; I finished the pasta, though the quantity was slightly more. It was tasty," said Ronny, relieved. "There is preparation to be done for the upcoming half yearly assessment," said Ronny as he reached for his school bag.

"Listen Darling, I am not suggesting that studies are not important or anything but 'all work and no play will make Ronny a dull boy'. I am wholeheartedly proud of your excellent grades but a healthy and active body is as important. You seldom go out and play," said Rose patiently. She knew admonition or a stern voice would be construed as being hostile.

"And this is your age…the growing years, to jump around, to sweat it out, that will keep you fit, energetic and lively in the long run. A habit instilled early on in life becomes a way of life. Once you reach adulthood, it becomes difficult to inculcate these vital habits."

"Ok Mom, but today I have too many assignments," complained Ronny. He picked up his school bag, hurriedly planted a fleeting peck on her cheek before heading to his room.

"And how is my brave boy today?" wondered Nashwin aloud, as they disengaged from a tight hug that, regardless of the tiring day at work, rejuvenated him instantly.

He worked as a Medical Representative for a reputed pharmaceutical company, which entailed visiting doctors, hospitals, nursing homes, etc. to promote company drugs and enroll them with attractive and sometimes unprofessional incentives if they prescribe them. The job required an ingratiating note, which irked him occasionally but as was with most things in life, he had gotten used to the job. His receding hairline was graying in discrete patches, accelerated by the hours under the sun while his tanned face stood apart from rest of his clear skin.

"How was school today?" he asked adoringly, planting a kiss.

"Normal dad," replied Ronny softly.

"What is the matter? You sound serious; did something happen at School today?" Nashwin straightened, concerned. His world revolved around his son.

"It's nothing. I am tired and feeling sleepy," he rubbed his eyes.

"Don't overstrain yourself Darling. You have to be fit to become a Pilot and more importantly you have to take care of your eyes," he advised, albeit he wanted to argue that excellent grades were not imperative to be a Pilot but restrained himself.

"Don't Pilots get bored confined to a cramped cockpit in the sky?" Ronny thought aloud.

"Not at all," his father countered excitedly. Nashwin's dream was shattered when his medical examination report in the final stages revealed an irregularity in his heartbeat, alienating the sky forever. The unfulfilled passion sprouted to life every time he saw Ronny who could have all the excitement he was denied.

"Just imagine the places you could visit, the thrill of cruising at seven hundred miles an hour at forty thousand feet above the ground," his eyes were beaming. He could imagine himself in a crisp shining white uniform with neat epaulettes and a peak cap, striding past a row of pretty air hostesses to the cockpit.

"Come on Nash, you still haven't freshened up; he has school tomorrow if you care. Dinner is served. You take your seat Ronny, Dad is coming," Rose was visibly irritated. The father-son duo yielded immediately.

"Hello Ronny," smirked Raj

"I don't want to talk to you," Ronny retorted.

"Are you looking forward to Mrs. Jones class today," he raised his sarcastic tone to include other classmates who were seated nearby. Several heads turned tentatively, but were not inclined to be drawn into a fracas, wary of Raj - the bully.

"Don't worry, Mrs. Jones will not pick you today," Raj giggled patronizingly, as he perched his arm on Ronny's shoulder. A few boys joined Raj, laughing in chorus. Another section of the class was transfixed to the spectacle.

Ronny jerked the arm away. His hands were trembling and eyes moistened with embarrassment on being abandoned, ditched by his class. He longed to punch Raj across his face but prudently decided against it.

"Good Morning class," the sudden announcement caused a flutter and the commotion metamorphosed into order with razor sharp accuracy.

The class Teacher briskly walked in, much to Ronny's relief. Miss Ratika gave a broad smile. She was delighted to start the day with her class.

The class boomed in unison, "Good Morning Miss."

Miss Ratika was around five two, with short hair neatly parted at an end and firmly clipped with an ornate pin at the other. She wore a sky blue cotton *sari* patched with small yellow flowers; its plaits flowed crisply as if they were ironed with starch. Miss Ratika gave the impression of an overgrown student at first look.

She placed the register on the table, surveyed the class cursorily and ordered them to settle down.

"Ronny! Come and see me during lunch. I want to have a word with you," said Mrs. Ratika, staring intently at him.

Ronny shifted nervously, unsure and gazed back with an empty expression.

"Say 'yes'," she said firmly.

"Yes," nodded Ronny weakly.

"Ok class, welcome back," she said tenderly, regaining her relaxed composure, "I hope everyone has completed their homework. Who hasn't?" she waited.

"Are you all sure? Ok," she continued. "I have some exciting news for you. Next week our School is hosting the Inter-School GK Competition, which is divided into two main categories - Primary and seniors. Don't worry about all that — our class belongs to the Primary group," Miss Ratika paused. She stopped pacing on the dais and looked at the class. All the students were hanging attentively to every word.

"And I have recommended Ronny and Raj from this class to represent our School in the Primary group," she smiled. "The remaining two will be picked from another section or class," she concluded.

"Anybody has a question till now?" she asked, sitting down on her chair behind the thick wooden desk.

"How many students are there from one class, Miss?" Dolly was up on her feet instantly.

"Each team has four participants - two from your class and two from another. We have twelve sections covering fourth and fifth grade to select the other two team-mates," she replied, teasingly mimicking Dolly's tone.

"When is the competition, Mam?" asked Raj.

"Seven schools are participating including ours. It is next Sunday, starting at eleven in the morning. Anything else you want to know?"

"Why on Sunday Mam? It's a holiday," asked Sammy naively.

"So that your parents, particularly your dad can attend dear," she answered sweetly.

All eyes were directed at Miss Ratika and though she occasionally displayed streaks of strictness and discipline, her soft caring nature with a veritable desire to teach made her students comfortable and interested.

"Ronny and Raj – your last period for the day during this week will be for the Quiz practice at the auditorium. Miss Susan will be there to guide and assist you," she said seriously.

"Miss," his voice was shaking.

"What is the matter Ronny?" Miss Ratika was taken aback.

"I don't want to take part in the Quiz," he blurted.

"What?" she exclaimed, bewildered. "Why?"

Ronny had not really shaped his reply to the question; how could he? It was all happening too fast. He stood there, glued to the ground, looking down.

Mrs. Ratika stood up; the creases on her forehead belied the mask of calm appearance that she had put on. She came down the dais near Ronny and propped his face at the chin.

"What is the matter dear?" she asked apprehensively. He was one of her favourite students, bright, obedient and chubby.

The silence in the class was deafening. Ronny stood his ground, making no endeavor to clear the air; the defiance elicited several murmurs across the room, which the class teacher silenced promptly.

The veneer of benevolence was being slowly eroded as the seconds ticked away. Miss Ratika waited impatiently for an opening, as Ronny groped in the dark for an appropriate explanation.

"Are you afraid or nervous on stage?" the class teacher broke the silence hoping to break the standoff.

Ronny looked up, hesitated briefly and shook his head.

"Don't worry child, even I am scared sometimes to be up there but you have to step up to conquer your fear, isn't it Ronny; you have to rise to the occasion, there is always the first time; there is no other avenue, no other option, but to go for it," Miss Ratika said sincerely.

"But…" he started.

"No buts," said the class teacher sternly, "I don't want to hear any whining or excuses from you. You will practice for the competition as decided and be there to make your School and us proud. Any doubt or questions?"

Ronny did not respond. His head was spinning in all directions like a top that keeps swirling once initiated. He did not want to contemplate how he would pull it off. He felt that the staring eyes were smothering him. He just wanted the bell to blast so that he could rush out to fill his lungs with fresh air.

"Raj, ensure that Ronny is there with you at the practice; you are a team now," she concluded emphatically.

"Ok, let's continue. We have a lot to cover today; everyone open your homework," said Miss Ratika, walking towards her chair.

Their eyes met. Raj showed his aslant teeth to Ronny's worried brows.

Concluding that after the decision in the morning, Miss Ratika must be done with him and would not be expecting him, Ronny skipped the lunch meeting with his class teacher that day.

He did not wait for Raj to exhort him and was the first to enter the auditorium for the practice, even before Miss Susan. He knew he had to play along. There seemed to be no alternative. The massive school auditorium with endless rows of reclining chairs fixed on a slope was one of the largest in the area. Ronny waited in one of the participant's chairs that were arranged to mimic the final setup.

Ronny desperately wished the dreaded week to breeze through but it dragged along, adding to his woes and anxiety. He had to pull himself up every day for the mock to avoid a showdown with Miss Ratika, who's headstrong and no nonsense attitude was capable of halting a raging bull in its track.

His low spirits would not spur even when brushed with Miss Susan's contagious exuberance. An unassailable authority on General Knowledge, current affairs, etc. coupled with a passion to teach, made her the right mentor to quickly brush up and refresh participant's rusty areas.

Raj's belligerence had mellowed and his feisty involvement in the practice reciprocated a simultaneous awe and irritation from his teammates. He could pull it off alone, thought Ronny with admiration.

"But it's a crucial day today," protested Rose.

Rose towered over the bed as Ronny lay with a contorted expression, ostensibly wriggling in terrible pain. He clutched his abdomen area with both hands drawing his knees to an embryonic position. Rose nudged him to bring him back. Ronny woke with a start and dropped back to a pillow, covering his face with another on finding his mother near the bed.

"What is the matter?" she frowned.

"I am not well. My stomach is in pain," he wailed.

"You must go for the competition; after all you have put in so much effort and time for it; don't let it just fritter away," she softened.

"Oh! But it's paining awfully," he groaned, tightening his grip on his abdomen.

"Don't worry Ronny, it will subside. You try to sit straight while I get you a fresh lime drink in warm water, which should do the trick. That will clear your passage and the pain will vanish," she said confidently.

"I don't want to go Mom, it's terrible; I will become a laughing stock for the audience," Ronny implored on the verge of sobbing.

"At least make an effort to get up. You are not a kid anymore," she lifted the pillow to reach his ears.

'If I were to request an extra hour of Internet, she would conveniently remind me that I was a kid,' thought Ronny

"What is the matter?" Nashwin barged in, unable to hold himself any longer, all the while being all ears, following the argument from his room and hoping it would ebb.

"He isn't well; wants to skip School today," she replied to the rhetorical question.

"What's wrong with my tiger," he sat beside Ronny and gently removed the pillow to uncover his face. He did not resist his father.

"I don't want to go to school today," he moaned, grasping Nashwin's hand, which immediately pushed the right buttons.

"He does not want to go today," he turned to Rose, as if he were a translator.

"I can see that," she said, looking hard at him. Rose could sense a fresh course of argument.

"So?" he wondered carefully.

"So what, Nash?" she countered, "He has to make an effort to at least try. The inter school quiz competition is a few hours away, that too in his own backyard. They have been preparing for more than a week now. Wouldn't it be an embarrassment?" Rose was visibly exasperated. "He would be letting down his teammates and the school."

"But none could foresee this; anyone can become ill suddenly. Our boy's health is our foremost priority, rest is immaterial and unimportant," he said with finality facing her.

"I know that; he is my child too, but inculcating certain standards of discipline is also critical, particularly at this age. He may have to muster monumental will power and conviction to make it today, but imagine the strength of character that he would develop. It will teach him to honour his word, no matter what," said Rose resolutely.

"He is only nine, in fourth standard; we don't have to be that harsh, it's only a kid's quiz competition. Come on," he slammed his palms on his thighs to stress the silliness of her argument.

"You are not listening to me; it's precisely because of his age I am pushing," she lost her calm and yelled.

As it normally happens during arguments, one compliments and effortlessly matches the other in animation, gradual rise in decibel and fury. Nashwin yelled back, "And are you listening to me, our child is sick and needs a doctor, not some personality enhancement lesson."

The real issue often, with alarming alacrity, becomes indistinct making it a personal tussle of ego and domination.

Nashwin continued as Rose glared at him, "Moreover, he is destined to become a Pilot, that is what he wants to be; these stupid quiz competitions are insignificant. Don't worry, there will be many more competitions like these"

"Oh God! Please don't start again with your Pilot rant. You have no clue how today might unfold, let alone what Ronny would be fifteen years hence. You are only clouding and baffling him with your unrealized ambition," Rose was exhausted.

She glanced at Ronny who sat wide-awake with his back resting on the headboard, apprehensive of the outcome. A fleeting idea that his affliction might be a charade crossed her mind. Nashwin thwarted it.

"Mind your words," he objected, pointing a finger at her. He was furious.

Rose glanced at the clock hanging on the wall opposite to Ronny bed; their scuffle had consumed more than half an hour. It was pointless to go on, she mused; he would be unable to make it on time for the bus. Nashwin was intently watching her for the next move while figuring a response in his head to her next move.

"When the School calls us for a meeting, for an explanation for his absence, which I assume could be as early as tomorrow, you better be present because I am not going to clarify or plead with excuses or toil to portray the universal notion that such quiz competition is irrelevant for the higher goal of becoming a Pilot," she said with calm sarcasm and walked out without caring for an affirmation.

Ronny was out of bed and looked out of his window as if unmindful of the altercation. The sun was bright outside; life bustled in a chaotic routine with people rapidly scurrying across the street like rats with a purpose.

His father came and stood beside him, gently playing with his soft hair.

"Are you alright, Ronny?" he asked softly. "Take rest; I have to go back to bed. It's Sunday, you know. I don't understand why they had to keep a competition today and spoil the only day we get for rest," yawning, he lazily strolled out of the room.

Ronny stood still. He prayed hard that he would not be called for a confrontation the next day.

'If anything has to go wrong, it will' or for that matter 'if anything has to go right, it will', as the adage goes.

The septuagenarian Principal sat straight beholding them. If his thick milky mane were dyed, it would have reduced his apparent age by a decade, maybe more. His wrinkled eyes, behind his round-rimmed golden spectacles, scrutinized the ensemble before him without divulging anything.

Having passed on the baton to a restive Nashwin who sat on the edge of his chair waiting for the Principal to break the ice, Rose appeared composed. Ronny stood between them while Miss Ratika and Miss Susan occupied the remaining chairs beside the Principle.

Father D'Souza leaned forward, placed both arms on the eighty-year-old Mahogany Desk; fingers entwined and said solemnly, "Mr. Xavier, Ronny is an outstanding, adorable lad and we are not here for retribution or to reprimand as the matter is not that grave but it still needs a resolution and some clarity."

Nashwin felt his muscles relax a bit and managed a weak, clumsy smile.

Father D'Souza spoke slowly, choosing each word with deliberation, "Quiz competitions are organized often and participating in one of them, if one is proficient becomes imperative and I must add that Ronny's team had to opt out due to his absence and that left them dejected while us, red-faced. Our main issue, however, is Ronny's overall attitude to the whole affair."

He paused to uncover the plastic lid and drink a gulp of water from the crystal glass kept to his right. He did not offer them any water.

"Miss Ratika claims that Ronny was disinclined to take part in the competition from the beginning and had said so when his name was first announced in the class. Did he show any such reservation to you?" he looked straight at the parents.

Nashwin turned and fixed his gaze at Rose as if it were her turn to answer. He was anyway clueless.

"No, we did not get any such indication from him. In fact I thought he was keen and enthusiastic about it," she said, coming to the edge of her chair.

"What makes you say so?" said Father D'Souza leaning back, his frame aslant, resting on one armrest.

"Well, after school, he would head straight to his room to study," contemplated Rose.

"But how did you conclude that he was looking forward to this particular event?" The Principal was calm.

"I reckoned he was; he loves to study, at times I have to forcefully close his books," Rose turned to her husband for support. Nash stared back blankly and nodded.

"That still does not answer my query. Let me assert that Miss Susan here recollects Ronny to be disconnected during the weeklong practice. She further states that he would come forth with an answer only when directly asked and not proactively. She felt that the boy was bright but somehow struggling...maybe unhappy... I don't know... that can be an area to prod, to uncover any fundamental complication or issues," Father D'Souza wondered.

"I think we are seriously straying from the crux of the matter. He was very sick that day, severe abdominal pain that can occur unannounced. Why are we making a mountain out of a molehill?" asked Nash genuinely.

"Mr. Xavier," the principal leaned forward again, his voice grave and countenance profound, "I don't like wasting anyone's time; least mine because as you can see I don't have much left; Let me be absolutely clear about one thing, the meeting is not about the quiz, we are not a run of the mill school, I am sure you would agree; but the meeting is about your child, who we agree, is not himself lately."

"Can you please elaborate?" said Rose who had been listening intently.

"We don't know. You have to tell us; are you a happy couple, you know what I mean?" asked the Principal cautiously.

"What?" exclaimed Nash after a lag when the implication sunk in, "Of course we are fine; I mean which couple does not squabble, but overall we are…. happy."

"Yes," concurred Rose. "We are fine."

"Hmmm," observed the Principal unsure of his next move.

"I think Ronny can make our predicament clear," said Miss Ratika for the first time. The colossal authority of father D'Souza often relegated other teachers, who were almost half a century younger to him.

The Principal nodded, stamping his acquiescence.

"Come here my child," Miss Ratika rose and gently pulled Ronny who all along had been bolted between his parents. She rubbed his back to ease the knots of discomfort that manifested on his grim face.

"Ronny, you have been listening attentively all this while and you know we all love you; but lately we feel you are sad, something is really poking you. What is it with my child?" she asked tenderly.

Ronny was looking down. He fidgeted as he trampled one shoe with the other. The dreaded moment had arrived; it had to someday though it came unexpectedly earlier and in an unfriendly ambience. There was no point in vacillating; he knew there was no escape.

The group patiently waited, drawing Ronny unconsciously to an impasse.

His Parents twisted uncomfortably to the left to keep Ronny in their view.

"Yes, Ronny?" urged Miss Ratika.

"Dad," he turned to address his father, "I cannot see clearly."

"What do you mean you cannot see?" Nashwin was totally attentive.

"I can see dad but not clearly from a distance…I mean the board is hazy from my seat in our classroom. I fail to make out the alphabets clearly," he quivered, barely audible. He spoke with his head bowed down.

"What?" exclaimed Nashwin incredulously.

The couple exchanged glances before Rose said, "Don't worry Ronny. We could have seen a doctor earlier if only you had shared. We will now."

"But what has this to do with the Quiz?" Nashwin was baffled. .

"It explains a lot I dare say," the Principal chipped in, "Ronny had known from the beginning that the competition would, for some rounds, require the participants to read the questions directly from the big screen fixed at one corner, farther away from them, which I presume due to his eye condition, made him anxious and was the source of his restlessness."

The Principal leaned back, his lips reshaped into an enigmatic smile as if he had just cracked a difficult case.

"You could have told us about it without fear. We will always love you, no matter what," Rose could not contain herself.

Ronny came closer to his father, his hero, with glistening eyes and said softly, "I am sorry dad. I would not be able to become a Pilot. I don't want to be a Pilot." He has failed his father, he thought.

The words hit Nash like a meteorite striking earth with unfathomable intensity.

When the mist cleared, Nashwin saw his son anew as if he hardly knew him and would have to begin afresh. He realized how his father, who continually strived to enforce the nobility of the medical profession citing its remuneration and honour, incited the dormant rebellion that made him an average pupil throughout his academic years. He could not muster the courage to share his dream of conquering the skies with his father. And moreover he forever blamed his father for killing his dreams.

He was exactly on the same path.

The severity of the damage, due to his own selfishness and insensitivity, that can last a lifetime and kill a germinating potential in its infancy made him shudder.

He realized why Ronny kept his condition buried. Like him, he did not want to hurt his father.

He rose from his chair and kneeled opposite to his son. Balancing on his toes, he affectionately drew him to a light embrace, their chest barely touching, and whispered, "I am sorry son. I forgot that being a Pilot was my dream. You have to choose yours."

Ronny could sense the lump in his father's throat. He moved forward, flung his arms around and locked his father in a tight embrace.

The Sober Love

"Strawberry MilkShake," she said, tossing the single page laminated Menu card towards him.

He picked it as a habit, gave a disinterested fleeting glance and threw it back.

"One strawberry Milk Shake and one err… coffee…" he smiled at the waiter.

"I guess the Menu has not been revised since inception," giggled Latika. She looked gorgeous in her fitting plain white *Kurta* with an embroidered neckline.

"This ancient Restaurant needs a makeover," remarked Aman, lighting a cigarette.

The open roof area of Kaventers, with its spectacular panorama of mountains in the background, the clock tower at one side and a languid commotion in the street below, typical to a tourist town, was a popular rendezvous among vacationers and locals alike. The place would invariably be packed for its popular non-vegetarian elaborate breakfast till before noon, easing off to a gradual flow of patriots during the day.

"Don't smoke here!" Latika exclaimed in a suppressed tone.

"No one is here except us; don't overreact," he said while carefully scrubbing excess ash from the tip with his index finger. He wore dark blue jeans and a white t-shirt with a symbol of 'Om' embroidered on its top left.

"And everyone knows me here," he added smugly, sucking hard on the rolled marijuana joint.

"Yes, everyone knows you smoke all the time. That does not imply you are free to smoke here," she retorted.

"I know dear…Ok! Here…." reconciled Aman. He stubbed the joint on the green parapet that encircled the roof area, before putting it back with other cigarettes. He reasoned that since he was comfortably high, cruising through the clouds, a couple of drags were enough. The ensuing argument would only be a spoiler.

He leaned back on the heavy wrought iron chair, his thin frame relaxed, arms perched loosely on the armrest, drooping eyes transfixed on something beyond, his bony face calm like an enlightened savant while Latika fidgeted impatiently for the milkshake to arrive or Aman to divert his intriguing eyes towards her.

The serenity, the mystery in his eyes and their capability to grasp her inner turmoil by the contours of her body language or expression had beguiled her that day.

"His name is Aman," said Jasmine handing a chilled Bacardi breezer, a mild alcoholic bottled drink popular with girls.

"So?" Latika rolled her eyeballs, feigning disinterest.

"I can get you introduced," prodded Jasmine, her slender finger circling the rough edges of the opening on the glass bottle.

Latika blushed while avoiding direct contact.

Although her brother Roshan, the principal architect of the evening, could be seen passionately entertaining his clique with their choicest booze, marijuana and psychedelic lyrics, the Soiree at Jasmines had peaked.

Close pals discretely occupied different pockets in the living room, some sitting while others on their feet, cigarettes dangling from their fingers, whisky glass in the other hand while the theme of the animated and occasionally raucous discussion was as diverse as Politics, music, AI, work or spirituality

"The place is becoming stuffy with smoke," observed Latika. "I am going to stand on the balcony for a while before I drop dead due to nicotine overdose or be smothered without oxygen. I just cannot stand these fumes, it makes my head spin. Are you coming?" she asked seriously.

"I desperately need a drag," winked Jasmine to her friend's annoyance. "You take the fresh air."

Latika walked out to the balcony.

"Hi, I am Aman."

Latika straightened, startled. She brushed aside her thick black hair from her small cute face to reveal her thin lips smeared with maroon lipstick. She was atypically tall at five seven, emphasized further by a fitting maroon overcoat and black jeans. She shook his skinny hand.

"Hi," she said, ending the awkward silence that had followed.

Aman sucked hard on his rolled joint, his thin artistic fingers maneuvering it with deftness like an artist rolling a paintbrush between his fingers. His long hair was neatly brushed back, the bunch tied back in a pony. With a loose T-shirt over his lanky frame, faded black denims and mustard leather shoes, he looked smart and clean.

"Did Jasmine send you here?" asked Latika, folding her arms together.

It was dark; the streetlight below sporadically caught a shadow, the interval between them increasing as the night progressed. Darjeeling retired early for the night, the cold compelling its inhabitants to snuggle into the warmth of their homes.

"She pointed to the beautiful lonely lady alone out on the chilly balcony, bored and something about how we can allow that in our rocking party?" explained Aman.

"I was not exactly bored; my eyes were burning due to the smoke," she smiled.

He crushed the cigarette butt with the tip of his leather shoes, took a deep breath and hesitated for a moment before speaking, "Would you like to go to a movie with me?"

The soft thud of the tray broke Latika's trance. Aman lazily gathered himself, pulled his coffee, added several sugar cubes and took a sip before slouching back again. He adjusted his woolen cap to cover his big ears, which he felt were frosting. There was no respite from the cold even in May; the tourists, on the other hand, arriving to the hill town in multitudes would have preferred the chill to continue forever.

"What?" asked Aman upon noticing Latika's gaze.

"Nothing. Don't smoke anymore, at least not until we are out of the house; you know how Mom feels about it and I don't want to give them fodder for concern," cautioned Latika.

Aman did not respond. He was flying with the cup of hot coffee in hand, away from his miseries. He crushed his point of view to prevent an inevitable quarrel. He might have to steal a couple of drags on the way, to help him sail through the evening, which he knew would be crammed with scrutinizing air, complaints, etc. If given a choice, he would have liked to be cloistered, surrounded by his paraphernalia, books or games.

But then, the monthly request was more of a command and hence unavoidable.

"How have you been?" asked Mrs. Vidhya Thapa without betraying any emotions.

"Fine," smiled Latika

"Don't lie to me. You look distraught. Don't forget I brought you up with these very hands," Mrs. Thapa raised her arms to underline her statement.

Vidhya guided her only child, the sparkle of her eyes inside after exchanging a few forced pleasantries with her son-in-law whom she utterly despised. Mr. Thapa, generally pliant, was directed to engage Aman with small talk.

"He is gradually improving. He needs some time," said Latika softly.

"Latika, it's been two years," said Vidhya moving closer, "I can see his blood shot dreamy eyes" she mocked further. "Maybe, to some extent, by being critical we have been responsible for the present estrangement. I know it has only made us drift apart, which was the last thing desired. But you tell me, how can we be a bystander, after all you are our only love."

Vidhya stopped to swallow the lump in her throat. She had vowed not to broach the subject, but the sight of her pale daughter and lazy son in law unbridled her emotions. How could she relax when her only child's future remained uncertain?

"Let's eat Mama, it's quite a walk from here to our place. I don't want you to worry about things that are beyond your control. I will use the wash room and join you guys," Latika planted a peck on her mother's forehead and left.

"You still have a chance," reminded Vidhya worryingly.

Vidhya had barged into her daughter's room, firmly requested her gang of buddies encircling her to excuse them and had taken the settee opposite her. Latika looked stunning in a violet Bhakhu, the traditional bridal wear with a golden decorative welt along the edges.

All attempts by Vidhya in the previous months to sway her daughter away from the marriage to a substance abuser as per her, had been futile. Latika had refused to even acknowledge her mother's concerns, let alone give it a serious brooding.

"God! Mama! You just don't give up," said Latika incredulously.

"Don't get married to that druggy. The whole town is aware of his habit. One thing you should be certain of, that being your

mother, I have your best interest at heart and it is my duty to show you the correct path or the challenges of your chosen road," said Vidhya resolutely.

"He has a name and it's not druggy," protested a tense Latika. "And he owns his own cab business, if I may remind you. Please give credit where it is due."

"Don't fritter away your life for nothing Latika; it's human to err but against the basic ethics of survival to jump into a well. Undoubtedly, you are mesmerized, in love and it's all genuine, I know, but you are blind to the turmoil that lay ahead," Vidhya was trying hard. She did not care if he were a millionaire.

"But all preparations are done; guests have arrived, more are on their way. What about society, our community?" Latika reasoned.

"Don't bother about anything dear. Relatives, friends are a dime a dozen; their agenda is quality of food, wine on offer; but your welfare is really not their priority. They will be well served, tittle-tattle briefly until another juicy topic grabs them. But the inevitable mess in your life ahead would be averted," said Vidhya with clarity.

"He will quit it all, he has promised," and as an afterthought she declared rather patronizingly, "I will make him sober, that is a promise."

The words hit Vidhya like a stray bullet in a battlefield, knocking her down. She knew her daughter to be radically stubborn to a fault on occasions but shutting all avenues of reason or communication with her parents on a decision that could alter the course of her life for worse was incomprehensible and regrettable. She sighed.

As she splashed hard, the blend of water and tears that had welled up scattered on the mirror, obscuring her reflection. She brushed her long silky hair, bunching them with a soft band and gave herself a final look of approval before joining her family at the table.

"How is your business, Aman?" asked Vidhya, trying hard to be pleasant.

"Its fine," said Aman.

"Aman is planning to buy one more Taxi," Latika chipped while biting on the chicken leg. She would have preferred Aman to keep mum.

"Why don't you resume your studies? Years flash by before one realizes that life is too short; you are young, hardly twenty-four, who knows you might get inspired to pursue Doctorate after Masters. The random lifestyle needs a new insight, a change of direction," the candid observation rattled Latika who stared hard at her mother.

"Yes, enrolling for Masters is worth consideration," concurred Mr. Thapa, speaking for the first time, trying to play down the insinuation.

Aman thwarted any attempts to get drawn into any conversation that he believed would culminate into an argument. He gobbled his food hastily, declined the offer of sweetmeats from Latika, excused himself inaudibly, strode to the adjoining room and switched on the TV to drown any noise coming from the dining area.

Latika relaxed and offered a silent prayer of gratitude that the evening had not spilled out of control. She was thankful that Aman had suppressed the urge to react.

"Why don't you divorce him?" grimaced Vidhya, nibbling at a chicken piece. She quashed the urge to be loud enough for her voice to reach the living room.

"I am going to bed. Are you coming?" yawned Latika.

"I will be there in a minute," said Aman, picking up a book.

"It's twelve, already late," she said, irritated.

"I know," he said, adding fuel to fire.

"You know! What else do you know? Do you know that you will probably sneak in at dawn and get up around noon? In a minute…. huh" snapped Latika, folding her arms and leaning at the door.

Aman sat on his favorite swivel chair in one corner of his small study room. The desktop on the thin wooden table in front of him was booting up. An alcove, within an arm's length, contained his entire contraption for the night. The wooden shelf on the opposite wall, behind his back, was overflowing with books on a multitude of subjects. One section was stacked with magazines. Barring the computer table and chair, the floor was covered with an old mattress wrapped with a clean sheet and a few cushions were strewn across. A Number of speakers, placed strategically for optimum sound effect and clarity, decorated the wall. On his left, a window opened to their balcony while on his right Latika stood menacingly, making him uneasy.

"Every morning or rather afternoon when you wake up, you promise yourself with such intensity and veracity your intention to bring your life to order, to quit your addiction, that it is shocking or rather disgusting to see your resolve blow away and become foggy like the very smoke from your lips as the evening unfolds. Every single day!" said Latika dejectedly. *'Stop it. It's not the right time for this debate. Go to sleep. Talk tomorrow,'* a voice cautioned inside her.

"What did your mother say?" Aman turned to her.

"My mother is not a part of our lives; let her be at peace" snapped Latika.

"When will she allow us some peace," murmured Aman under his breath.

"What? What did you say?" Latika straightened. *'Stop it, I say. He is high.'*

"Nothing," he looked towards the window.

"I heard what you said," she persisted.

"Listen dear, the day we visit your folks, why do we end up bickering till dawn?" he said plainly.

"She only has our best interest in mind," said Latika defensively.

"Best Interest. Huh! Has she ever spoken nicely to me? Since the day we got married, she has only belittled me. So, she did instigate you." smirked Aman.

"There is nothing to instigate; the only reason I am confronting you is that it is affecting me, not because my mother has an unfavorable opinion; I don't care whether she is fond of you or not, but at least I should be comfortable and peaceful," she inched forward.

"So, you are not happy; is that what you are saying?" said Aman casually, emptying a cigarette.

"I am disconcerted; I am frustrated," she said grimly.

"Has your love for me dried up?" said Aman looking straight.

"Did I say that?" she frowned.

"There is no point in a protracted argument which I know is not going to yield anything. I understand that you would like me to sober up; though I had not promised anything about quitting ever, before or after marriage, but believe me, I am trying," said Aman while filling an empty cigarette with weed.

"I can see that," she ridiculed.

"But do I bother you; Am I abusive or dominating or dependent or what?" he leaned back on his easy chair, savoring the first puff. *'How can I quit this magical flower,'* he lamented inside.

She pulled a hard plastic chair from the dining area and sat facing him, maintaining an adequate distance to avoid inhaling the poison as far as possible. Aman glared at her, making his displeasure clear.

"Aman, this cannot go on. I hate our frequent squabbles, but your attitude towards your addiction is really annoying me lately. Far from being accommodating of my views, you deem it unnecessary to talk about it. It's been two years since our marriage and now I get the feeling that you don't intend to quit," her eyes were transfixed on a paperweight on the table. Her lips trembled as she spoke.

"Am I bothering anyone; my business is fine, you know we are getting another vehicle; I am popular in this town, my friends like me; we often go to parties, at least once a week, like before. I don't see where the problem lies," he reasoned, mimicking her graveness.

"For heaven's sake! You grope for a joint first thing in the morning and remain doped till you hit the bed. You are an addict! You need help!" she yelled.

"But I am doing fine in life. I am neither a liability nor a junkie who needs rehabilitation. And for your information, this stuff is legal in many countries across the globe," the high elicited an induced tranquility in his manner that further infuriated Latika.

"For your information, it's not legal here. And I don't care if it's being distributed for free all over the town. What I know is that you are losing it, spiraling down with superfast speed and it is making me crazy," she lamented.

"You are overreacting. I love marijuana. The stuff really fuels my imagination and I am not losing my mind," he said passionately.

"Overreacting! I get an eerie feeling that you didn't listen to a single word of what I said. We don't have a goal, no shared enthusiasm, nothing to work for; we are just dragging along. Even ants works as a colony with a sense of purpose, the game of survival spur them to go beyond, to explore," she said, bending forward, trying hard.

"But we are surviving," said Aman, reaching for his cigarettes.

His words outraged and repulsed her. Ignoring her parent's trepidation, she had married an exuberant, feisty Aman who used to be full of life, who dreamt of making a difference, an extraordinary person with diverse ideas to create something beautiful. But the spirit within the flesh and bone before her was decaying; it was caged in a fortress of addiction, breeding dreariness, mediocrity and abject insensitiveness for others.

Aman turned to the screen as a gory figure came alive on it. His right palm gripped the mouse deftly, as he avidly maneuvered the protagonist on his noble mission to recapture the nuclear island, spilling blood and decimating an army of adversaries who dared cross his path. The level of passion he displayed for those frivolous games fascinated and saddened her at the same time. *'He is blind to his immense potential'*, she thought.

"I don't think I would be able to walk together much further as things stand now," she said softly.

Aman looked up, his drooping eyes measuring her. He paused the game and asked, "What do you mean?"

"You know what I mean. Our game is over, I guess," she said plainly.

The resolution in her voice unsettled him. She had not ever in all their innumerable fights displayed such calm demeanor or candour.

"I think you are tired. I have vowed to complete this stage today and I need to concentrate. Let's discuss tomorrow and I told you I am trying," he tapped a key to resume his adventure.

Latika left the room.

The heavy cast iron bench, rusted at several spots, tilted awkwardly to one side making it uncomfortable to sit for long without frequently adjusting one's position. A few ragamuffins with light bamboo sticks in their hands cavorted at a distance, poking at each other while the youngest among them, barely a couple of years old, continuously shrieked with excitement, trying to catch his older peers with outstretched hands.

Latika had removed her snickers, pulled her legs up and snugged at one corner of the bench; her left arm rested on the slender armrest, taking some weight off her tilted posture. She had six hours to squander before embarking on an introspective phase as the train to Kolkata was scheduled to depart at seven in the evening.

Her wheeled blue duffel with retractable handle, stuffed with clothes lay in front.

Aman,

Please understand the insecurity and chaos that has filled my mind with noise so intense that it's imperative for me to be away, to declutter and have a definite design for the future. With or without you is the key question. Maybe our life is perfect according to you, but I am miserable if you ask me. I have to think hard. I am leaving to be with a friend in Kolkata, who has promised to accommodate me temporarily. My next communication will definitely have clarity.

Latika

At dawn, around six when cabs to *Siliguri* had started plying, she quietly sneaked out. Aman would anyway not notice her absence until noon. The departure note was pinned with an ornamental magnet on the fridge.

"Can I share the bench?" a soft voice startled Latika, bringing her back to the railway platform. She instantly lowered her legs and straightened herself to make space for the old lady.

The frail woman carefully sat on the bench, turned to Latika and smiled. Her silver hair was neatly tied in a bun while her wrinkled grin on a bony face and robust plastic spectacles made her adorable. She radiated an uncanny amiability through her deep compassionate eyes. Latika guessed she must be above seventy or maybe more.

The old lady fumbled with her brown handbag that she had kept by her side.

"Sandwich?" the woman stretched her arm, holding an opened red tiffin box.

Latika hesitated briefly before picking a butter sandwich, which was neatly manicured at the edges.

"Are you travelling alone?" asked Latika after taking a swig from her water bottle.

"Yes," said the woman.

"Where?" asked Latika, hoping to strike a conversation.

"Kolkata," the old woman replied, her mouth stuffed with bread as she chewed endlessly.

"Me too. You have company now," smiled Latika after a while.

"Why don't you answer it?" the old woman said. Latika's cell phone would come alive intermittently with a high-pitched tune that reverberated through the tranquil and quiet afternoon. The railway platform was deserted except for a few poor travellers who were sleeping at a distance on dirty sheets. Several half naked children teased each other at the other end.

"I don't feel like talking," said Latika dubiously.

"But you are talking to me," the woman smiled.

"To him, I meant," said Latika.

"Him?" the old woman prodded.

"My Husband," Latika hesitated.

Aman had called a dozen times since eleven. If she answered, the conversation would conclude with acrimony and severe heartache, she felt. She needed to seriously contemplate before engaging him.

"Do you stay in Kolkata…or visiting someone?" asked Latika to steer the chat.

"Visiting. My Ex-husband," she smiled.

Latika remained silent as another push in that direction might be viewed as prying. *She does seem fit for her age,* observed Latika. Dark green veins protruded like a maze on the back of her palm as she rested on the bench, staring ahead in deep thought.

"He lives in a mental asylum there," the old woman continued after an extended pause, "for the past forty years. I visit him twice a year, tomorrow being one of those days, his birthday, though he will not recognize me, never has in all these years," she said calmly without any misgivings.

The candor, elegance and level of personal sharing took Latika aback. She had expected a casual small talk; the profound revelation stumped her.

"It must have been hard for you and your children," Latika treaded cautiously, not knowing what to say.

"Why do you think so?" she asked.

"Well…" stumbled Latika.

"I found a great man who lit my life with love and care. He has ensured that my children do not miss their father for the last forty years. They adore him," she said with pride.

"You visit your husband alone, I mean your children don't accompany you," Latika was feeling comfortable with the lady, given her level of comfort with the topic.

"No, they don't remember him or share any connection," she said as if it were normal.

Latika remained silent. Here was a woman, who conscientiously visited her erstwhile husband although he was incapable of either appreciating it or even cared if she existed. She was bewildered.

"You see," she continued on seeing Latika's perplexed countenance, "he has an affliction, not me; he is miserable, not me; but you know what, when I am with him for an hour, twice a year, I can see the sparkle in his eyes, a calmness in his being, an unsaid gratitude which overwhelms me and brings forth a deluge of memories that indisputably are one of the most joyous that I have. Though we don't utter a single word, fresh camaraderie blossoms each time we meet; we inexplicably depart rejuvenated."

"Should I not endeavor to ensure a moment of joy for the person I love?" she smiled.

Latika was too enamored to respond. It was noble.

"I am only loving the person I love, nothing great," she added softly, looking ahead.

It was almost six and the street kids had vanished. Sunlight was waning out.

Passengers for the train to Kolkata had started trickling in and the number of local mobile vendors on the platform, offering tea, coffee, cold drink, ice cream, cigarettes, etc. rose steadily. The loudspeaker blared regularly with updates on several trains that were due to arrive or depart later during the evening.

The old lady had closed her eyes to unwind while Latika sat still, feeling restive as a tiny sense of indecisiveness poked at her.

The magnitude of relevance in her own life in what the old lady said suddenly exploded inside Latika as she stared at her. She was turning her back on Aman, who was her world, who was the reason for her moods, who was the only confidante she had. Here was a woman who travelled five hundred kilometers to elicit a smile from a person who has lost the ability to reciprocate. The depth of the old lady's generosity made her shudder.

Does she really love Aman?

What is love after all? Is it the possibility of realization of a life that you imagine as worthy or comfortable that drives your love for your partner? Is it focusing on reshaping or rewiring your partner to your layers of perception? Or is love just an expedient arrangement to survive together?

Isn't true love supposed to be unconditional? Latika stifled the dreaded answer that was beginning to take form.

"Have I really loved Aman in the last couple of years without searching for a reason to love?"

A zealous focus to sober him robbed them of their free expression while pushing Aman to his shell. After marriage, her world has been dominated by a single pointed focus to coerce Aman to give up on his addiction.

'You are not his mother,' the thought jolted her, sending a shiver down her straight spine. *'What is the difference between you and your mother?'* a voice demanded, tearing her apart. *'Both of you sound the same to him.'*

How could he listen to what she said, when her voice, ever flavored with righteousness, was unable to pierce his defensive walls? How could he divulge his goal or desire without the fear of ridicule or sarcasm?

Maybe Aman has a great vision for them, she thought. That he loved her was undeniable.

Maybe eventually they would part ways but it would be after she had offered her soul to her partner, after she had given all to their relationship, after she had experienced love with him.

Aman would have no choice but to love her back. She smiled contently as a small drop of tear scratched her cheek. She could clearly see how her life would unfold.

Her phone buzzed.

"You should answer it. I think he is missing you," smiled the old woman.

"I have," smiled Latika, "and thank you," she kissed the old lady's hand. "I have to be somewhere urgently. I am sorry but you will have to travel to Kolkata alone."

"I told you, I always have," she smiled back.

The Silence

My frail grandfather was stretched out before me, his head raised against the post, his upper back curved and his wrinkled eyelids shut. His ribs undulated against the thin cotton vest as he breathed. Around eighty-five, a few strands of white hair sprouted from above his ears on his otherwise shiny scalp, his sunken cheeks made conspicuous by his toothless jaw.

He was my cousin grandfather, my grandfather's younger brother but I was particularly close to him, like some relationships that don't require a gestation period to be comfortable, like flammable vapours attracting a spark; it's instantaneous. More than a decade ago, during my college days, I visited him quarterly on a Sunday and we had quickly developed a mutual admiration. Aged around seventy-two then, he would zealously welcome me and we would explore and dissect myriad topics from state of Indian or International Politics, Cricket, Cinema, Food, health, ways to a woman's heart and more often than not, I would be listening to daring tales from his prime when he was a young, spirited officer in the forest department. After lunch of fish curry and rice, my grandmother would retire for her siesta and we would be lazily perched in the living room, him on his easy chair and me opposite him on a single sofa.

With a cigarette clipped between his spindly fingers, legs crossed, and interspersed with frequent guffaws, he often held me enthralled with a fresh escapade like when a baby elephant had fallen into the netted ditch planted by poachers and how he and his team, along with the encircling tuskers had toiled for eighteen hours to resurface the calf with coconut ropes and stitched gunny bags.

Convincing the giants to pull on the ropes was effortless, intelligent as they are, he would observe casually. He could have spoken telepathically to them if needed as he often did with some other species; he said emphatically squinting his eyes, which off course I did not believe but let it pass. The clan, needless to say, raised their trunks in unison to a trumpet call like a royal cannon salute. When finished, I would cheer in amazement his indomitable spirit and courage.

Sometimes a bout of incessant coughing would grip him like an epileptic attack. I would watch helplessly as the grating fit would engulf his body, his mouth buried inside a towel, eyes bloodied and watery while his free hand tightly clasping the armrest. He would walk haphazardly in between the furniture, his back curved, his throat unrelenting. Often he would vanish out through the front door, probably out of embarrassment and to soak in some fresh air.

You should quit now, I would casually remark later. He would chuckle knowingly, showing his four remaining teeth and shrugging away my concern. Curvy wrinkles would emanate from the edges of his gleaming eyes, swirling around his cheeks in an ornate pattern. Like a laughing Buddha, his face would glow with life as if the intense discomfort a moment ago was in a distant past. Every moment is to be lived fully; he would remind me calmly as he often did, whether in pain or pleasure. They would pass in a blink like life itself.

I would snigger reactively and pull out a couple of sticks from his packet. "Take more", he would insist and I would tap out a couple of more and carefully slide it inside my pack. With limited resources during college days, cigarettes would eternally be short and any generosity would be shamelessly accepted. On my way back to college, I would empty one, stuff it with crushed marijuana and take long drags and exhale slowly to milk the last drop of potency. The world around me would slow down as if to match my frequency. I would stride past the evening bustle, hands pushed inside black trousers, my nose catching the pungent aroma of the evening incense burning somewhere, my heavy eyes devouring the intense world with a hazy but arrogant gaze. Sipping sugary tea at one of the roadside *Dhaba*, a wooden structure with a slanting tin roof and earthy floor, I would light a cigarette, the cloud of smoke hitting my throat, burning its way down the windpipe. Someone would brazenly light a *chillum* beside me, raise the smoking deity to his forehead as veneration, suck menacingly at it and pass it across to his eager comrade.

The frenzy before me continued unabated, pedestrians, rickshaws, vehicles crisscrossed ceaselessly in a sort of precise orderliness, like a designed chaos. I would stare distantly thinking about the day well spent, about the glint on my grandfather's eyes, his loud wicked laughter, his exuberant chatter or his firm handshake. Unlike other weekends, when I would be with my friends, this would stand apart with a mysterious sense of fulfillment like best buddies who meet after ages. It would be several months before I would be seeing him again and I knew he would be waiting, hoping that I would turn up sooner.

I curved my chest out and pulled my arms to the back for a protracted stretch. The old man had not moved an inch. It was already a long tiring day compared to my otherwise indistinguishable and relaxed routine as Chief Engineer on board *MT Azure Trader*. Previous day our vessel had docked at *Haldia*, a lackluster and medium sized Port approximately 130 Km from *Kolkata*. Unloading of fifty thousand metric tons of Vegetable Oil brought from Indonesia was in progress while I, after delegating the reins of technical responsibility to the second engineer, had taken a day off to visit my old folks in *Kolkata*. My wife, Vani who was sailing with me, a prerogative of a select few on merchant ships depending on seniority, had insisted the night before that we make the trip and after an initial hopeless attempt to preserve my languid pace, I had yielded half-heartedly.

We had stepped down the gangway at seven in the morning to a waiting cab and clear sky. The driver was a heavy man with a bulging belly that stretched his checked half shirt to its limits, a round face with thick drooping moustache and flattering manners. As we approached, he bowed perfunctorily while grinning broadly to reveal his tobacco-stained teeth.

The small town was quickly left behind and we were breezing past verdant paddy fields on either side of the highway. A few bent figures, like statues, their *lungi* pulled up to their knees and tucked to their waist, were scattered across, immersed in their land. A hay figure with outstretched arms and a football crudely painted to resemble a human was secured to a tall bamboo stick to scare predatory birds

A straight smooth road, pleasant February wind caressing our dry skins, cruising speed and a FM station churning melodious yesteryear's evergreen numbers uplifted me like an excited child who has spotted an ice-cream vendor. Not a bad idea after all, this outing, I thought. Vani looked elegant in traditional *Patiala Salwar-Kurta* and bangles. It was her first visit to my old folks and a get-up, commensurate with their preference would instantly impress them, an overused but effective maneuver to get a direct entry into their good books.

After a quick breakfast at one of the popular highway stops, we arrived at a little past eleven.

'He doesn't talk much these days. Not all it,' my grandmother had said plainly after the initial pleasantries. Her white hair neatly parted at the center twisted into an enormous bun at the back. She looked fresh in spite of the burden and exertions of the past couple of years.

'He was hospitalized last week. The doctors said his lungs were full of water. He was also frequently breathless and had to be ventilated,' my aunt, who had remained unmarried, sat erect by the side. She was a frail woman with a small face and tanned skin.

I nodded assimilating the details. His condition had been in a mess since the debilitating fall two years back when he had slipped in the bathroom, landing precariously on his left hip bone, fracturing it irreparably. After months of immobility, he was prescribed a walker to start walking with slow baby steps around the house. The doctors had promised that after a few months of sustained practice, he would be able to quicken his pace with support. The reassembled pelvis will strengthen over time for him to discard the aid, they assured him.

He had hated the contraption from his first endeavour. It reminded him of his incapacitation, his sudden loss of freedom and his banishment to a slow painful wait for the end. More than anything, his bloated patriarchal pride was punctured, as he was rendered useless, an object to be taken care of without any say in his small world which he had nurtured like an autocrat. Not that he had been averse to opinions or suggestions - they were crucial to not allow the other members to slip into oblivion, which would mean without a subject, but the final verdict had always been his.

As days progressed, he had pushed away the walker, resigned to his condition, and pinned himself to the bed. On days he would be utterly cantankerous, demanding cigarettes, or a particular dish that he would later refuse to eat, hurling biting criticism or expletives at the one unfortunate to be in his vicinity, which mostly would be his wife.

On rare occasions, he would wake up charged, with that unmistakable sparkle in his eyes, a resolve to conquer his misery and an enthusiasm to bury the past and surge anew. He would demand his favourite dish, gulp protein shakes, rattle away like a baby who enjoys the sound of her voice and be ruthless with his walker. Within a few hours resignation would creep in and the euphoria would plunge like a hit warplane. For days, he would fasten himself to his bed, rarely putting his foot down, talking to the silence in the room. For the past six months, a stout woman with a large face and perfect teeth has been employed who would carry his wasted frame like an infant. She is the only one who had been spared his biting scorn, I am told.

His back had been raised against the wooden post after we had arrived and he had laboriously opened his eyes, deep curvy ridges forming on his forehead. His thin lips stretched on one side to a welcoming smile and his eyes slowly brightened to the same luminescence that had captivated me for years. I was visiting him after five years and first time since my marriage.

My wife touched his feet and he gestured to her to sit beside him on the bed. I sat on the chair in front while my grandmother and aunt stood near the wooden cabinet.

He was visibly excited to see us, grinning and chuckling away at his playful and lively attempt at pulling my leg. He showered effusive praises on Vani who sat demurely like a bashful doll while grinning to his every wry humour directed at me. Laxmi later claimed that she had not seen him so spirited before as if suddenly life had been pumped into him through a magic wand.

He dispatched Laxmi to prepare tea for everyone like a child who is unconcerned with others' preferences.

'Don't listen to him. He has always been stupid,' he gave a frail wicked smile to Vani who giggled as if being tickled all over, something to get back at me at an opportune moment.

'When is your ship leaving?' he abruptly turned to me.

'Tonight… maybe early morning,' I said. 'I will leave by evening', I added quickly as if reading his mind.

He did not respond and if he had any emotions, it was hard to say as he looked blankly. Probably he was expecting me to stay longer for us to have a chance for a real conversation as old friends meeting after a long hiatus or he was mortified to portray his waning state, frail and attenuated body and that he wished us to leave sooner.

I could see a glimmer of sadness in his eyes in not being able to jump in enthusiasm and fervor on seeing his old pal separated in age by half a century. He managed a weak smile but his eyes shone with enthusiasm.

'Lunch?' my grandmother broke the silence looking at my wife.

'I have brought a protein shake; it's a good one, the most expensive one in the market. It will give you energy,' I said, hoping to revive him.

Gently, he curved back to allow his head to find his soft pillow and closed his eyes.

He did not speak again that afternoon.

After Lunch of plain rice, steamed fish in mustard paste and mixed vegetables, I sat beside him on his favourite easy chair that had broad curved teak armrests. I could hear my wife chatting with my grandmother and aunt in the adjoining room, analyzing the minutiae of a local recipe.

'He rarely speaks these days,' said Laxmi who was sitting on a cane stool just outside the room.

I nodded, unable to offer an appropriate response.

I was jerked to my senses by a slight tap on my shoulders. Vani stood with a cup of steaming tea and some biscuits. I had dozed off for half an hour. I yawned lazily before grabbing the cup.

A gilded clock adorned the azure wall opposite the heavy teak bed. The position of its black needles made me confirm the time on my mobile. It was indeed fifteen past five - time to leave.

I touched his forehead. I was sure he was awake but he did not make any attempt to open his eyes.

'He is driving like crazy,' I said casually, holding my Nokia a little away from my damp ears. My senior on the other end of the line continued his bitter tirade against one of our colleague whose systematic and brazen embezzlement of the organization's assets had recently come to light. His fiery words blared into my ear from a distance. We were back on the highway, flying in fact, after squeezing through the rush hour traffic of Kolkata.

My wife, Vani nodded reflexively, as she concentrated on the dark highway from between the two front seats of the cab. Her eyebrows were slightly raised, pulling the eyelids along with it, stretching her small eyes. Her round face appeared tense; her expression wooden; understandably so, as the car raced past another truck and swerved to the left, barely missing a sedan speeding toward us. My heart skipped a beat.

'Can you please hold on for a second Sir?' I spoke abruptly, cutting the flow of words.

'Oh… Ok… any problem?' he said after a second, probably taken aback.

'One second Sir,' I urged and pressed the phone on my thighs to somehow cover the microphone and block my voice from reaching the other side as if I were going to say some secret. Why we do that intuitively I still haven't figured it out.

'*Bhai*, we have time… this is not a racing track,' tapping on the driver's flabby shoulder, I hinted jokingly at his reckless driving. I leaned forward to bring my mouth closer to his ear.

'Don't worry Sir, I have been driving since the age of fourteen,' he yelled proudly above the engine's vroom as if that gave him some kind of invincibility and he further slammed the accelerator. 'I know every inch of this highway,' he boasted in his throaty voice. For a moment, I mused giving a firm order to slow down, but immediately vetoed it. I did not want to hurt his feelings, not that I knew him personally or anything, in fact, we had only met in the morning, but that is how I was I suppose, genial and pliant. Moreover, my cell phone, dug onto my spindly thighs with my superior presumably waiting on the other end was yelling for my attention.

Vani was at the edge of the white leather seat, not blatantly nervous but mildly apprehensive. Our eyes met momentarily, I stared blankly not knowing what to utter while she pursed her lips to disapprove of my timid protest and the unruly cabbie. She immediately turned her attention to the road to forewarn herself at the slightest clue of danger. With our vehicle zooming past to overtake every movable object in front of us, winding and zigzagging to whiz past with total disregard to traffic rules, she would not get time to yell. I too would have been fixed to the windshield were it not for the phone, so I lazily slumped back on the seat and brought the device to my ear.

'Sorry Sir....' I began apologetically.

He straightaway commenced his rant against the disgraced colleague like a movie in continuation after a popcorn break in cinemas. I gazed out through the raised windowpane. The line of halogen poles on the central divider was blanked out and we had entered a dark patch of the highway. I was staring into blackness. A truck crossed us from the opposite direction, its pair of powerful beam, lighting us up, blinding me for a moment.

'Watch Out!' my wife screamed, her voice pierced the air as if she was directly aiming at my eardrum.

Instantly I lifted myself up or I did not, I don't exactly recall. I thought I saw something ahead, a pair of beams or an enormous irregular boulder or a concrete wall, but that was my mind, conjuring images from memory, objects I might have imagined crashing into in the past.

It happened so swiftly that I don't even remember hitting anything and passing out. I remember the cold steel of the metal on my ear, my eyes devoured by the blackness and then nothing.

Pairs of eyes, almost popping out of their sockets, were intently focused on me all around the wooden table. I saw a few more squinting at me from behind them. The ensemble was responding to my slight movement as if we were synchronized in a wavy interference. I looked around. A fuzzy woman with a miserable expression was staring at me. I could not place her or anyone towering over me in that thatched shed with a solitary naked bulb hanging over us. I felt a sharp pain somewhere in my head. I staggered as I pushed the wooden table to stand and instinctively pulled my left hand as I felt a piercing pain in my left wrist. I must have cracked something there. Several hands lunged forward to grab me from falling and I was pushed down into the safe confines of a plastic chair.

'Where am I?' I said with a frown, my eyes quizzically probed the countless eyes staring at me.

'Why am I here? What is happening?' I demanded nervously. The eyes continued to stare as if magnetized.

Suddenly the gloomy woman was near me. I looked up. She was saying something but I could not hear as if my ear was deflecting the sound vibrations or the brain was incapable of processing. My panic rose with every passing second. I could see amazement intensify in the intrigued faces gathered around me, which increased the muddle raging inside me.

I stood abruptly, fear completely overpowering me. 'What is happening?' I sound desperate. 'Who am I?'

The woman grabs my arm as I flounder clumsily. 'We had an accident. Are you ok?' she says, deep lines of worry running parallel on her forehead.

'Accident? I want to go home.' I turned, trying to extricate myself from her.

'We were going to the ship,' she said, coming closer.

'Ship?' Nothing made sense. 'Why are we going to the ship?'

'You work on a ship. Our ship is about to leave in a few hours. We had an accident. A big accident,' she claimed seriously. The urgency in her tone was clear.

Slowly I settled on the only chair and faced the sea of people who had not budged and were bending expectantly for an opening. I wedged my elbows on the coarse wooden table and buried my face inside my palms. I was getting restless and annoyed with the confusion. A soft hand touched the back of my neck and slowly travelled across my shoulder. I eased a bit as the hand slowly increased the pressure on my shoulder blade in a gentle circular motion while a cool breeze brushed against the sweat on my chest through the unbuttoned shirt. The pain on the head resurfaced, but I was too entangled with my identity and existence to focus on it.

'We were going to the ship," my mind echoed the woman's voice.

Suddenly in a flash, without a precursor, a deluge of past gushed from all directions into the abysmal reservoir of my mind. The empty canvas was rapidly filled, with each successive image becoming clearer. It all came back to me, my identity taking shape to assert my presence like a compass that swirls uncontrollably but settles pointing north. That identity gives a sense of security but ties one down to fixed patterns and expectations.

'Oh', I exclaimed. 'I have to go back to the ship', I uncoiled like a spring, straightening up. 'We had an accident. How?' I asked no one in particular. I gently dabbed the top of my head with my fingers, finally able to locate the seat of the pain. My fingers turned red and wet with blood. My body now cared more for the pain that was insignificant up till that moment. I looked at my left wrist. The pain was nagging without any visible sign of injury.

'So we had an accident,' I grinned. Accidents can become amusing if your injuries are trivial.

Most of the faces grinned in unison breathing a sigh of relief. They were all clad in a *lungi* raised to the knees and their chocolate chests were bare. As I was told later that they were the locals who had rushed to the site on hearing the loud bang of the collision and had broken the rear windshield to pull me out swiftly. The rear doors were allegedly jammed and I was blacked out for me make it to the front. Rear exit was more practical, they had reasoned after a quick consultation.

I turned around to see Vani manage a tentative smile. She was clearly tormented. Her hands were still resting on my shoulder. I got up and embraced her. I could only imagine the severity of the accident as I looked at the crushed steel where the bonnet had rammed to align with the front windshield. My wife recalled that our vehicle smashed head-on into a car parked innocuously on the muddy stretch away from the road. The innocent driver was on his phone when we literally flew into him, catching him off guard. His injuries were severe enough to be rushed to the nearest hospital, which was an hour away. Our car had, as I was excitedly explained by one of my saviours, become vertical after the impact and spun several times on its hind before landing on its side, its wheels still turning. People from the nearby village on the highway, quickly restored the car's stability and dragged me out like a troop trained to deal with highway accidents.

'You were unconscious for more than fifteen minutes. I was so scared,' Vani said. We had moved a little away from the crowd that had considerably thinned since I regained my bearing.

'Are you alright?' I asked, holding her hand.

She nodded. She had miraculously escaped unhurt apart from a few superficial bruises on her shin.

'Where is the driver?'

'He is missing. Nothing happened to him. He saw it coming just in time I guess and he also had his belt on. Crazy asshole,' the anger in her voice did not surprise me. She can be opinionated, I knew.

'You should go to a hospital,' one of them closed in to interrupt us.

'Where is it?' I asked.

'Around an hour from here, maybe more,' he offered, scratching his temple.

'Forget it. I have to be on the ship within two hours if I have to leave with it and I want to leave with it,' I said bluntly, looking at my wife. 'I have already called my agent. He is sending another cab that should be here in an hour,' I informed him, hoping he will convey it to his comrades.

'My house is just across the road. You can wait there. You can have tea and we can apply some Dettol on your cut,' he said pointing to his head.

'My cab is on its way. We are....'

'It's cold outside. Don't worry. We will keep a lookout for your cab,' he insisted.

The house was a modest single story rectangular structure, its facade painted in some light colour, which I could not specify in the dark. Beyond the house I could make out the lush fields, covered in darkness.

We entered into an average hall and were directed to an oval dining table that had a glossy veneer with four wooden chairs around it. An old greying man with a white flowing beard and a rosary in his right palm sat on one of the chairs. A fair lad of probably fourteen or fifteen, with a long face, full lips and a deep gaze smiled at us as we took the remaining two chairs. Few men who had entered after us settled on the lone sofa in one corner.

Someone placed tea before us in small tapering corrugated glasses. No one spoke. I managed a faint smile. The pain in the head was rising. Someone brought a small bundle of cotton and a half filled bottle of Dettol as if reading my mind. I asked Vani to investigate the wound and apply the antiseptic. She was on her feet in an instant.

'You should get a checkup done in a hospital. It's an hour from here, the nearest one,' the old man said with a deep concern, his fingers caressing the beads. His big eyes dug into mine waiting for a reply.

'I am fine. I have to go to the ship. The cab will be here in a moment,' I blurted clumsily, sounding stupid.

The old man closed his eyes and went back to his beads.

Vani had cleaned the deep cut and temporarily bandaged it. I will have a relook on the ship I consoled myself.

I took a sip of the tea. It was loaded with sugar, like syrup.

Seated before us, the young boy, in his teens, fair skin, thick hair, and a handsome face, continued to smile. I smiled back unsurely. He was making me uncomfortable with his sugary expression. The crowd had thinned by now, baring a couple of men who buried themselves in a newspaper. I felt tired, as if the cells in my body were suddenly reminded of an exceptionally eventful day that had begun at four in the morning. I crossed my arms over the table and buried my head in them. My back and shoulder muscles ached from tiredness and impact.

His hands were soft and gentle. His fingers skillfully dug into my aching muscles of the back, slowly traversing the uneven surface. I groaned in relief, which encouraged him to gradually increase the pressure. I lifted my head with my eyes closed and rested my back against the wooden backrest, insinuating to him that he should focus at the base of my neck and across my shoulders, which he gladly obliged. His tireless fingers continued their magic, slowly untying the intricate knots of my muscles. I swayed my neck from one angle to another, relishing the divine massage.

After what seemed an eon, I opened my eyes, straightened my back and turned around. The boy was smiling. I smiled back, this time effortlessly. He pulled a cane stool and sat beside me, the smile not leaving his baby face even once.

'Thank you,' I wanted to say but it seemed too insignificant compared to his magnanimity. The unexpected massage to a stranger was filled with love and kindness. The more I looked at him, the more his palpable warmth enchanted me.

'That was excellent. Thank you,' I could not manage anything more lavish.

The boy smiled. His eyes were unwavering, locked into mine.

'What is your name?' I smiled, clutching my left wrist that had started to hurt.

He smiled. It was as if he had been punished to smile.

'The massage was really good. Great! You must be in school,' words were drying up and I was not able to keep up with the smile.

'He cannot speak. And cannot hear,' the old man looked up, his big eyes unblinking.

'What?' I gasped incredulously. The old man did not smile. My focus shifted from Vani to the old man. How can nature be so cruel with this loving being, I wanted to protest.

I turned to the boy. He was smiling, his eyes shining with clarity. Words have to flow through the eyes and be understood with a smile. My sympathetic expression gradually rearranged into a smile of warmth that one feels when truly connected to another human being.

What advice do you give to a deaf and dumb person? Get well soon or try some other treatment. To communicate you have to be one with him. There is no other way.

Suddenly there was nothing to say or do but just be in the company of each other. Relish the moment and celebrate the union with silence.

My grandfather's wrinkled face flashed across my mind. I knew I would not see him again. Why had I gone to visit him? Because he was a dying relative or had I gone to meet someone I cherished.

And it dawned on me that I had blown away my chance of celebrating our friendship that afternoon. What he desired was not some dull remedy to get on his feet. He did not want to get on his feet. He only wanted to celebrate the union with me. There was nothing to say.

'The cab is here,' someone announced at the door.

I nodded. Vani was the first one to be up on her feet. I pushed the table with my right arm to support my legs as I stood up. The smiling teenage Buddha stood up with me, his fingers entwined.

The old man gestured a faint goodbye with a quick blink. I pulled out all the notes from my wallet and smiled at the boy. He declined profusely, lips widening to a grin. I insisted and thrust the wad into his soft hands. He shook his head and glanced sideways at his grandfather who signaled his approval.

A silent goodbye; Strangely, I did not feel the urge to speak. You relish the togetherness and part with a smile, both parties in full awareness of the briefness of the moment. It was much simpler, like being connected at the core where words have no meaning.

After bowing to each other's smiles, I walked out through the open door into the cold wintry night.

The Unspoken Distance

"I want to go out!" yelled Naisha, fruitlessly pulling at her mother's right arm with all her tender might. Karla did not budge an inch.

"It's too hot outside. I will take you in the evening," Karla offered, sitting down on the English rolled arm sofa. The daily afternoon ritual was playing out.

Naisha could sense the annoyance in her mother's voice, one of her inflexible tones, which blocked any attempt at persuasion. She ambled barefoot to the parapet and stretched her toes on the small wooden stool, straining her neck to get a better view of the ground below. She lived on the first floor of the apartment. Anil sat lazily on the mound of hot sand, sifting it through his tiny fingers.

Naisha was conspicuously taller than most infants of her age; she had turned two and a half a few days back, her soft silky hair, trimmed to just above her eyebrows, flowed uniformly like the shining strands of a Japanese doll. The big eyes on her small chubby face twinkled as tiny sparks of mischievous ideas formed inside her small head. As a toddler with a clean slate, she possessed an inordinate appetite for life and its experiences.

"Anil is playing outside.... with sand...see Mama...see," she crooned in her cute manner from the balcony, the exuberance in her voice though infectious, failed to nudge Karla. She ran back to her mother as if the stern denial a moment ago had not happened. "Mama!" she pulled.

"Let him play. It is too hot outside. We will go in the evening," repeated Karla, slowly edging towards anger. The dreadful Delhi summer was stealthily approaching with the heat typically stronger for the first week of May. Karla was in her late thirties, though a distant acquaintance or stranger would have confidently gambled it to be early thirties. Karla worked out vigorously, drank lots of water for her skin and ate prudently and sparingly to keep fit.

"I want to play with Anil!"

"Not now."

"Owwaannhhh," exploded Naisha, her tiny lips widened to incredible proportions, covering almost the entire face. "I want to play with Anil," she managed to shriek through her gaping mouth without moving her lips as tears streamed down her pink cheeks in abundance.

"Don't cry, baby," Karla softened, the sudden outburst taking her unaware. She pulled Naisha to her and wiped the channel of tears with her palm. "I have something for my darling!" she sang desperately.

But the child was inconsolable. The lure of "something", obscure and not clearly defined, failed to divert her from the tangible pull of soiling herself on the mountain of sand. She yelled more as if the agony was becoming unbearable.

Karla stood up and took the child in her lap, slowly rocking her. The rhythmic sway combined with her mother's warm embrace soothed Naisha briefly, distracting her from her priority.

To Karla's discomfort the protest resumed with renewed vigour a moment later.

"Ok, Ok we will go," she said grimly, eventually caving in.

"Now?" beamed Naisha, the acrimony transformed into joy in a flash like a dog's effusiveness on his master's arrival in the evening.

She ran to get her favourite pair of shoes.

"Don't go that side, it's dirty…. doggy shit," shouted Karla. "Not that side, I said," she repeated, the heat and a stubborn child were making her utterly restive. Love for her daughter gave her the impetus to brave the scorching sun at four in the afternoon.

"Come…come…Anil…come this side," chirped Naisha, pulling her friend.

"Softy Naisha…. he is a baby… pull softly, he might get hurt," intervened her mother.

Anil grinned at the sky. With dark brown skin, a small cute face on a tiny body and a conspicuous paunch, he was almost a year younger to Naisha. His well-oiled hair was tied behind in a ponytail and he frequently smiled at Naisha or Karla, showing his couple of mini teeth. He sat leisurely on the sand, smeared with it, his abode for the day, unmindful of the blistering Sun or the dirt around.

Seeing Naisha in the evening, he would become animated and approve of her presence by frequently thumping on the sand with his palm. It was a friendship that transcended words, a human connect that was ethereal and alive. It was pure, a friendship based on nothing, no approval, caste, colour or even a desire for a friend. It demanded nothing except the presence of the friend. And it encompassed everything in that moment as it was based purely in the moment, for the moment.

His mother appeared from inside the house that was being constructed and stood beside Anil. Laxmi's dark face was dripping with sweat. Her bright *Sari* was wrapped around her head till her eyebrows. She removed the cotton towel that was rolled as a cushion to ferry bricks on her head and wiped her face. Her only prized possession, ornate gold earrings, adorned her ears while her nose was pierced with a plain silver ring.

She greeted Karla with an exaggerated bow, her respect bordered on reverence. For Laxmi, Karla represented an echelon of society that she could not and must not aspire to match. In Karla's presence, the glaring and outrageous economic disparity overwhelmed her, making her reticent, timid while the difference in skin color made her cringe and reminded her that God so wished it to be. Maybe in the next birth, they told her, if in this life she could complete the required list of good deeds to qualify for that luxury.

She could be one attractive lady if groomed, thought Karla; *outstanding if a bit fairer*, she added to her thought.

Both mothers stood watchful as their children frolicked in the sand, an integral part of the construction material where Laxmi and her husband laboured as daily wage workers. Karla's face would occasionally light up with a smile or nod in acknowledgment as neighbours strolled by or when Naisha captured her attention with her exuberant antics. Naisha busily made tunnels, structures, and cakes in the sand, and with a mighty roar she flattened them and remoulded them into new creations. Anil, enthralled by his vivacious young companion, roared with laughter and cheered joyously at her every move.

"Mama, let's go to Anil's house," said Naisha, finally weary of the antics on the sand.

"Look at yourself. You are filled with sand. Look at your hair," scolded Karla.

As Naisha stretched, tilted her neck and rolled her eyeballs, attempting to get a glimpse of her soiled hair, she stumbled, to be caught by her mother in the nick of time.

"Come here," groaned Karla, as she vigorously scrubbed her daughter with a hand towel to dislodge the yellow granules.

"I want to go to Anil's house," repeated Naisha, indifferent to the wobble.

To Karla's dislike, Naisha was fascinated with Anil's house and for the past week insisted on following Anil to his house.

"Ok...Ok...let me clean you first," frowned Karla.

A rough-hewn cottage stood in a far corner adjacent to the structure under construction. The walls were made of loose un-cemented bricks piled on top of each other, and the flat decrepit canvas roof was fastened to a brick at each of the four corners. The bricks consisted of numerous gaping holes inviting fresh air, mosquitoes, an inquisitive rat or a bold squirrel. The tiny area that would be bereft of breathing space if more than three adults attempted to make themselves at home was floored with a torn mattress at one end, an old rusty metallic fan and a pile of clothes dumped on an aluminum trunk at the other corner. A single bulb, powered through a temporary connection tapped illegally from a nearby pole, hung at the centre of the canvas cover.

"Don't worry Madam, I will take care of *Guria*," said Laxmi, lifting her son to her lap.

"Ok," agreed Karla grudgingly. "But bring her back. She will be hungry after some time. And it will be dark very soon."

Naisha immediately grabbed Laxmi's outstretched finger before her mother could change her mind.

A few steps and a split second later, they were at Anil's front door. Laxmi placed her son softly on the temporary platform drawn out of bricks that was filled with sand at the edges and on top to make it relatively soft—an open-air sitting room. She brought the only stool from inside and offered it to Naisha while she made herself comfortable on the bricks. Anil crawled a couple of steps to Naisha's feet and offered his patched teddy, the stuffed toy whose white cloth was concealed under a layer of grime and dust. Laxmi sat with the kids, one on the stool and the other on the ground.

Naisha would not budge from the cane stool that was appropriate for her height; her feet firmly touched the ground, unlike the chairs at her home, and that really thrilled her. Strangely, while in their company, in Anil's bare living room, for the past few days, without any communication or maybe the need for it, Naisha would be transformed from a hyper, restive infant to an epitome of composure and serenity. She just remained on the stool as if it were heavenly.

As the sky turned greyish, just before enveloping the town in darkness, Ram, Anil's father, a skinny labour, literally devoid of any body fat, appeared. He carried two packets of fun-clips, tiny puffed cheese balls, in his hand.

"Naisha only wants to be with that Labourer's kid," said Karla casually.

She was laying the table for two after putting her daughter to bed.

"What labourer's kid?" asked Ruben while glaring at the TV remote for a button that he could not find. He wore cotton shorts with a sleeveless vest.

"A young couple work as construction labourers at the new house that is coming up next door. The whole day, their son, around one and a half, is literally on his own under the merciless sun, engaging himself with whatever comes his way - mud, sand, stones. These 'low class kids' are really hardy," observed Karla, wiping a plate.

"Hmmm…they are…yes," concurred Ruben. He found the key on the remote.

"And our stubborn kid loves to be with him in the evening or outside his shack," complained Karla, wiping sweat beads from her forehead with the back of her hand.

"Infants love to explore; what we may call a 'mess', is an exploration or a decoration of the finest quality for them.

Perhaps the laborer's son's display of unbridled freedom is captivating to her, alluring her away from the confines of our class.

A child knows no bound, no class; a child is free," observed Ruben philosophically.

"I don't mind Naisha spending some time with Anil. I know she loves to soil herself in that dirty sand, the glint in her eyes while picking up the stones or kicking the mud is unmistakable. I want her to be free; let her be free, after all what awaits her in this world is a demanding journey to continuously get better and brighter," Karla contemplated knowingly. She came and sat beside Ruben.

"What is the matter then? Any way she will grow out of it sooner than you realize," wondered Ruben aloud, feeling his thick moustache with a finger.

"It's just that occasionally she comes home with a packet of fun-clips - you know those cheese balls. I guess they offer her out of courtesy since their son loves it…or maybe it's cheap…. I do not know. She is a visitor to their… err… house… after all.

But the point is that she devours the packet with single-minded focus, more so since we seldom indulge her with junk food. And as a consequence, she loses her appetite and refuses to eat her dinner. Anyway it's a herculean task coaxing her to eat and unattainable if she does not cooperate," rued Karla.

"It happens sometimes," dismissed Ruben, fiddling with the remote.

"She slept today without eating anything; just that packet of useless balls. It has happened twice now," charged Karla, irritated.

"Then tell that lady not give it to your daughter," Ruben was unperturbed.

"I had told her the first time itself," retorted Karla.

"Then tell her not to bring the stuff in the first place itself," suggested Ruben.

"How can I demand that? They might love giving it to their son!" said Karla, rejecting the advice.

"Then don't send Naisha to play there," said Ruben trying to read something on the screen and that infuriated Karla.

"You are not even listening. If that were an option we would not be having this elaborate discussion. You have no idea about the ferocity of her tantrum if I don't agree to take her," claimed Karla.

"Or you can persuade her to play with other kids, our neighbour's kid – Ishaan; he is a cute boy…isn't he?" said Ruben indifferently. The crisis in the Middle East seemed far more immediate and worthy of his attention than his wife's predicament.

"God! Ruben, I told you, she just wants to run to the labourer's kid," exclaimed Karla raising her arms.

"What do you want me to do?" Ruben turned to face her.

"Nothing. Don't bother. Just watch that stupid news," mocked Karla.

"No seriously!" he repeated.

"Do you want to watch TV or should we have dinner?" the cynicism in her voice was clear.

"Laxmi, please don't give that packet of fun-clips to Naisha when she comes to play with Anil. She loses her appetite and does not eat her dinner," Karla requested firmly.

Karla had sneaked out in the morning to quickly share her mind with Laxmi before Naisha woke up. Anil was busy on his personal mountain.

Laxmi nodded. Any request from Karla was akin to command for Laxmi.

The glaring disparity in the living conditions of the two neighboring women was nothing short of scandalous - one fighting tooth and nail for a meager meal, while the other indulged in abundance. It was as if a massive spaceship has transported an entire race from a far-off dying planet, and these destitute beings scattered on earth were struggling to subsist in an unfamiliar, alien world.

After sunset, Naisha barged inside her house with a half empty pack of cheese balls, her stuffed mouth causing both cheeks to bulge out. Her eyes shone with excitement.

Karla fumed.

"Did my darling eat her dinner today?" asked Ruben from his fixed position in front of the TV, scratching his balls vigorously through his shorts.

"I snatched the packet that she was cheerfully brandishing. She got so upset with me that she wouldn't stop howling until I gave it back to her. And as usual she became uninterested in her dinner and I had to run after her all over the place with a rice bowl. She ate a little bit," said Karla worryingly.

"Hmmm," pondered Ruben.

"And why do you always have to scratch your balls?" said Karla, coming near him.

"It's a guy thing. I could have requested you to do it for me, as you seem interested but then the mighty Lord designed it such that real satisfaction could only be experienced when a man labours to scratch himself, " grinned Ruben as he scratched brazenly.

"In your sweet dreams, I would never be interested in this disgusting habit," frowned Karla.

"Did you talk to the woman about the packet? Is she beautiful?" winked Ruben.

"What is wrong with you today? You are repulsive," grimaced Karla.

"Just because she is poor, it becomes revolting to admire her beauty. Are they not human? If it were some cine celebrity, it would not only have been acceptable but proper to laud his handsomeness. Right? Such hypocrisy is not uncommon," mocked Ruben.

"I don't want to argue with you," said Karla, not liking the direction of the discussion.

"So did you talk to her?" smiled Ruben.

"Tomorrow I shall make it absolutely clear to her," said Karla resolutely.

"I told you yesterday not to give anything to the baby," confronted Karla. It was more of a question that demanded an apology along with a genuine explanation, than a statement. Karla had decided to pay a visit to Anil's Spartan dwelling.

Naisha was comfortable on her favourite stool, ostensibly hers every evening for an hour. She had a thin bamboo stick in her hand to dig up mud at will. *'She wouldn't sit for a moment at a place in the house and look at her here'*, thought Karla.

Anil sat straight on the bricks with a loose t-shirt, his dusty bare legs spread apart. It was from among Naisha's old clothes donated by Karla a few days back.

Laxmi sat beside them kneading the flour into dough for chapattis for their dinner. A heavy griddle lay in front of her on a makeshift brick oven.

Some labourers including her husband washed their hands and feet at a distance with water stored in a large plastic drum. It was six in the evening, the day's work was over but the Sun was a long way off from going down.

Laxmi looked up to reveal deep eyes that have ridden the tempest innumerably, a life entangled with hardship at every step.

She is pretty, noticed Karla again.

"She loves them, Madam," smiled Laxmi, showing her yellow teeth. There cannot be a better reason to give, she thought.

"I know," snapped Karla. She was in no mood for a discussion on the issue. She knew what was best for her child. Period. "She doesn't eat her food after that."

Laxmi shook her head. Karla's harsh expression brought the point home and moreover, she was absolutely clear about her limits.

"Let's go baby, it's dinner time," said Karla turning to Naisha, who had been listening keenly to her mother, dreading the moment she would be asked to leave.

"I am not hungry," she tweeted in a sad tone.

"Let's go, I said," Karla repeated

"I want to play with Anil," she tried another reason.

"It's late. And it's dinnertime. Let's go," she ordered.

'I don't want to go," she pleaded.

"Do you want me to take you by force?" Karla was running out of patience.

"I want to play with Anil," Naisha had exhausted all her alibis.

Ram, who had been wandering at a distance for a while, an uncouth, ill-bred commoner, was hesitant to approach his temporary home to avoid Karla. He strode swiftly inside his shack and emerged a moment later. He picked up his son, who chuckled sweetly. He nodded a quick salute to Karla without looking up. Karla, whose eyes had been fixed on Naisha, straightened with a frown. The situation had suddenly turned awkward for her. Ram handed a packet of cheese balls to his son, placed him softly on the hard stone, and walked away without a word, diffusing the tense air and unknowingly creating another.

"I will take him inside," said Laxmi nervously, aware of the repulsive look on Karla's face.

"Couldn't your husband wait for another five minutes? What is the rush to feed this trash to his child? He should have avoided bringing it to the baby's notice when I have warned you so many times," Karla was agitated and uncontrollable.

"Anil is hungry. Maybe he thought…" She knew her husband had waited patiently for a while.

"Then give him something nutritious," snubbed Karla

"Anil eats rice in the afternoon. Being under the sun the whole day, he becomes too tired and cranky by evening and revolts if we attempt to feed him. Someone told us that it is good…puffed rice with cheese – at least he eats something," Laxmi was out of breath. It was more than she had spoken the entire day.

The glee on Anil's face as he displayed the packet to his mother with a chuckle, probably urging her to tear it open, turned into a high-pitched wail as Naisha dashed from her stool and snatched it from his tiny fingers.

"Give it back to Anil," Karla yelled immediately, embarrassed.

Naisha gripped the small packet tightly, holding it close to her chest as if it were her favourite toy. On his mother's lap, Anil continued to howl, pointing at the bright packet.

The humidity, the apparent embarrassment and her desperation to liberate herself of the situation made Karla sweat profusely as if wild cats had besieged her. She quelled the urge to slap her daughter.

"It is Ok Madam, she is a baby," said Laxmi meekly.

"No, it is not Ok," bellowed Karla. She hated being out of control.

Karla lunged at her daughter and pulled hard at the blessed packet. Surprised and annoyed at the firmness of her hold, she tugged harder with all her might to split the thin plastic packet, spilling the precious yellow puffed balls all over the place.

"Hell!" she cursed.

In a fit of rage, with both hands, she lifted Naisha, who screamed and resisted her mother with all her might, and stomped towards her home. Each violent step dislodged a few balls, adorning the path from Anil's house to Naisha's with a trail of puffed gems. As the distance between the two friends increased, Anil's cries faded into the background.

Unnoticed in the distance, Ram stood with his head bowed, a fine film of tears blurring his vision.

Ruben abstained from poking into his wife's cantankerous and irritable mood. With one look at her contorted expression, as if her doctor had declared that she would never be able to lose that extra fat on her belly, his discerning mind clearly sensed the gravity of the situation. He knew she would be fine by morning. He kissed his daughter, who slept peacefully on her wooden cot and headed towards his favourite spot during that time of the evening.

Naisha never demanded to play with Anil after that wild evening. She relinquished control to her loving mother, knowing as they say infants do, at a very deeper level, that none other than their mother loved them unconditionally and had their well-being as a priority.

Occasionally she would point to him in the evening while she tried to mingle with the 'neat' kids of the block. Anil would turn his back on noticing her, hold his mother tightly and look the other way. Laxmi would listlessly encourage her son to greet Naisha, but the scared child remained adamant.

"Would you like to play with Anil?" Karla smiled. She regretted her wild temper the other day and the fact that Naisha no longer demanded to play with him. She could sense a sudden loss of feistiness in her daughter. Naisha would be fine; she consoled herself.

Naisha gazed into the void, a fleeting expression of melancholy, perceptible only to an astute observer, flickered across her face. She knew that Anil was not eager to receive her. She glanced at her mother, and with a gentle tug, led her to a band of children playing with a football.

Naisha, the two year old toddler was now aware of the hierarchy in her world.

*Born in Jaipur, **Shashanka Ghosh** was raised in several cities from north to east India.*

After graduating with a B. Tech degree in Marine Engineering from Kolkata in 1997, he followed the natural step forward and joined Merchant Navy as an Engineer.

In a career spanning more than twenty years, rising up the ranks, shashanka eventually got promoted to Chief Engineer in 2008, the highest position in the field.

Reading has been a passion and the urge to pen down his own stories has always been there.

Shashanka is married and stays with his wife and a daughter in Faridabad, Haryana.